Slow Cooking & Casseroles

Slow Cooking & Casseroles

Edited by Anna Horn

STERLING
INNOVATION
A Division of Sterling Publishing Co., Inc.
New York

Library of Congress Cataloging-in-Publication Data Available

2 4 6 8 10 9 7 5 3 1

Published in 2007 by Sterling Publishing Co., Inc.
387 Park Avenue South, New York, NY 10016
Originally published as *Quick Cooks' Kitchen: One-Dish Meals*

Portions of book are comprised of material from the following Sterling titles:
The Ultimate Casserole Cookbook © 2002 by Sterling Publishing Co., Inc.
The Ultimate Slow Cooker Cookbook © 2001 by Carol Heding Munson

© 2004 by Sterling Publishing Co., Inc.
Distributed in Canada by Sterling Publishing
c/o Canadian Manda Group, 165 Dufferin Street
Toronto, Ontario, Canada M6K 3H6
Distributed in the United Kingdom by GMC Distribution Services
Castle Place, 166 High Street, Lewes, East Sussex, England BN7 1XU
Distributed in Australia by Capricorn Link (Australia) Pty. Ltd.
P.O. Box 704, Windsor, NSW 2756, Australia

Design by Liz Trovato

Photographs by Evan Bracken
Food Prep & Styling: David Rowland & Scott Schronce

Sterling ISBN-13: 978-1-4027-4350-4
ISBN-10: 1-4027-4350-5

For information about custom editions, special sales, premium and
corporate purchases, please contact Sterling Special Sales
Department at 800-805-5489 or specialsales@sterlingpub.com.

Contents

Introduction

With so many options for a quick meal—quality frozen, prepped and ready-to-heat foods; take-out and delivery; and microwavable everything—there seems to be little reason to cook! Do you, however, long for the aromas and flavors of home-cooked meals? *Slow Cooking & Casseroles* provides you with 174 recipes that are full of homemade goodness to satisfy the busy chef in us all.

The recipes in *Slow Cooking & Casseroles* contain an eclectic mix of flavors. From regional specialties to gourmet delights, the recipes offer delectable savory tastes for the simplest and the most educated of palates. Such a claim can rarely be made and fulfilled, but with the ease of preparing casseroles, stews, and other one-dish treats, it is possible.

The roots of one-dish meals go back through every generation and to every ethnic background. These recipes remain staples for basic reasons: They provoke the emotions of comfort, warmth, and security; and the ingredients need only to be combined in one vessel—a pot, Dutch oven, casserole dish, or sauté pan—which makes prep and cleanup a snap.

One-dish meals combine more than two or three ingredients, cooked in the oven or on the stovetop, and are usually served in the same dish in which they are prepared. They can be baked in containers in a wide variety of sizes, shapes, and materials.

When choosing casseroles, baking dishes, and stew pots, the heaviest are usually the best. The heaviest-gauge pans spread and hold the heat evenly, thereby cooking the contents evenly. They also will last longer and have a tendency not to warp. Casseroles with lids are very helpful. Glass casseroles or baking dishes may be covered with aluminum foil for the oven and plastic wrap for the refrigerator, but lids are preferable with other materials. Below are descriptions of a variety of materials used for casseroles, Dutch ovens, baking dishes, and pans.

Cast iron

Some cooks believe a cast-iron skillet is a must in the kitchen to get the old fashioned flavors they remember from mother or grandmother. Cast iron is a very good material for cooking because it cooks evenly and it can go from the stovetop to the oven.

Copper

Copper is the chef's delight and usually left to the professionals because of the expense. Besides looking great and cooking evenly, it's undeniably the best type of pan. They're great if you can afford them.

Coated Aluminum

Heavy-duty aluminum with non-stick coatings (which eventually do wear out despite of the manufacturer's claims) are very popular because they are reasonably priced, lightweight, and cook evenly. Those that are anodized are stronger and will probably last longer.

Stainless Steel

Stainless steel is one step up from anodized aluminum in terms of appearance. All good stainless steel pans have a layer of copper or aluminum on the bottom and sides or a layer sandwiched between the coatings of stainless steel. Make sure they are heavy and not lightweight.

Enameled iron

Enameled iron puts a pretty face on a plain pan. The more expensive ones have the qualities needed for cooking, but also the outside attractiveness needed for the dinner table.

Ceramic

Ceramic- or porcelain-coated metal falls into the same category as enameled iron. It was created for its attractiveness at the table. Just make sure the metal properties meet your needs.

Glass

Glass pans are probably the least expensive and most widely used. It's the dish you'll use for most family meals and pot-luck dinners. If it gets broken or lost during the cleanup it can be easily replaced.

If you could only choose three sizes, you might consider the 8 x 12-inch rectangular pan, the 9 x 13-inch rectangular pan, and the 9-inch square pan. If you could just have one, the 9 x 13-inch would have to be the first choice. Its general all-purpose size and shape

hold most of the casseroles found in this book.

Casserole Containers

7 x 11 x 2 yields 6 to 8 cups
9 x 9 x 2 yields 10 cups
9 x 13 x 2 yields 15 cups

Sauce Pans

Small: 1 to 2 cups
Medium: 6 cups (1^1/$_2$ quarts, 1.1 L)
Large: 16 cups (4 quarts, 4.4 L)
Note: It's important for all pots and pans to have lids.

Cooks' Tips

Efficiency shouldn't equate frenzy: Always have a game plan or strategy for each recipe that will help to keep you calm. If you are wondering how you can put a meal on your table with relative ease—here are some tips:

• Read the recipe from start to finish before beginning your prep. Make sure you understand the directions and reread anything that seems unclear to you.

• Start by getting all your ingredients within reach and do all your prep work before beginning to cook. That way, you can cruise through the instructions and create a super one-dish meal.

• Use store-bought broth and beans. Many of these canned goods contain high sodium content, so check for low-sodium products and rinse your canned beans before cooking.

Pasta & Rice Favorites

PREP TIME: 15 MINUTES   COOKING TIME: 10 MINUTES

Zucchini Fettuccini

MAKES 4 TO 6 SERVINGS

This vegetarian dish features a rich sauce and delicate vegetables. Garnish with hot pepper flakes if you prefer a spicier flavor.

12-ounce package fettuccini
8-ounce carton heavy cream
8 ounces fresh mushrooms, sliced
1 stick butter sliced in half
3 to 4 zucchini, cut into 2 1/2-inch strips
1/3 cup grated Parmesan cheese
1/3 cup chopped fresh parsley
1/2 teaspoon seasoned salt
1/4 teaspoon white pepper

- Cook fettuccini as directed on package; drain. Toss with 1/4 cup cream. Sauté mushrooms in 1/2 stick butter. Add zucchini, remaining cream, and remaining butter.

- Heat, cover, and simmer for about 3 minutes. Add cooked pasta to mushroom-zucchini mixture. Toss with Parmesan cheese and parsley; mix well.

- Spoon into a buttered 3-quart baking dish. Heat at 325° for about 10 minutes.

Vegetable Lasagna

MAKES 6 SERVINGS

The only reason you need a head start on this delicious lasagna is because it needs to chill for 8 hours: It is easy to put together because you do not have to cook the lasagna noodles. It's well worth the 8-hour wait.

1 4$^{1/2}$-ounce can Italian-style stewed tomatoes

1$^{2/3}$ cups pasta sauce

2 cups nonfat cottage cheese

$^{3/4}$ cup grated Parmesan cheese

$^{1/4}$ teaspoon salt

$^{1/4}$ teaspoon white pepper

9 lasagna noodles, uncooked, divided

4 zucchini, shredded, divided

7 1-ounce provolone cheese slices, cut into
    strips, divided

● Stir together stewed tomatoes and pasta sauce. Set aside. Stir together cottage cheese, Parmesan cheese, salt, and white pepper.

● Spoon one-third of tomato mixture into a greased 9 x13-inch baking dish. Place 3 uncooked lasagna noodles over tomato mixture and top with one-third of the grated zucchini. Spoon one-third of cheese mixture over zucchini and top with one-third of provolone cheese strips.

● Repeat layering procedure twice. Cover and chill at least 8 hours. Remove from refrigerator and let stand for 30 minutes. Bake covered at 350° for 45 minutes. Uncover and bake additional 20 minutes. Let rest 15 minutes before serving.

PREP TIME: 20 MINUTES   COOKING TIME: 40 MINUTES

Cheesy Spinach Manicotti

MAKES 6 SERVINGS

This cheese-lover's manicotti is a great dish for family or company. Add a green salad with an Italian dressing and you have dinner!

1 tablespoon oil

1 large onion, chopped

1/2 cup chopped green bell pepper

2 garlic cloves, finely chopped

16 ounces ricotta cheese

1 1/2 cups shredded mozzarella cheese, divided

3-ounce package cream cheese, softened

1/2 cup grated Parmesan cheese, divided

1 tablespoon Italian seasoning

1/2 teaspoon seasoned salt

1/2 teaspoon black pepper

10-ounce package frozen chopped spinach, thawed

8 manicotti shells, cooked, drained

26 ounces spaghetti sauce

● In a skillet, heat oil until hot. Add the onion, bell pepper, and garlic and sauté; set aside. In mixing bowl, combine the ricotta, 3/4 cup mozzarella, cream cheese, half the Parmesan cheese, and the seasonings; beat until smooth.

● Drain the spinach well by squeezing between paper towels. Combine onion mixture with the cheese mixture and spinach, mixing well. Spoon mixture into cooked manicotti shells.

● Pour half the spaghetti sauce into a well greased 9 x 13-inch baking dish. Arrange shells over spaghetti sauce, then pour remaining sauce over the top of manicotti shells. Bake covered at 350° for 30 minutes.

● Uncover and sprinkle remaining mozzarella cheese and Parmesan cheese over top. Bake another 5 minutes until cheese has melted. Serve immediately.

PREP TIME: 25 MINUTES   COOKING TIME: 1 HOUR 10 MINUTES

Italian Dinner

MAKES 8 SERVINGS

Baked Italian dishes are famous for their rich flavorful sauces, bursting with herbal flavor. This recipe tastes wonderful on the first night, and even better as leftovers.

2 pounds lean ground round beef

1 onion, chopped

1 sweet red bell pepper, chopped

2 ribs celery, chopped

2 garlic cloves, finely minced

32-ounce jar spaghetti sauce

3 6-ounce jars sliced mushrooms, drained

3/4 teaspoon ground oregano

1/2 teaspoon Italian seasoning

Salt and pepper to taste

8-ounce package medium egg noodles

8-ounce package cream cheese, softened

1 pint sour cream

1 cup grated Parmesan cheese

16-ounce package shredded mozzarella cheese

• In a very large skillet, brown beef, onion, bell pepper, celery, and garlic; drain. Add the spaghetti sauce, mushrooms, and seasonings. Heat to boiling, turn heat down, and simmer for about 15 minutes.

• Cook noodles according to package directions; drain. With mixer or hand beater, beat cream cheese until creamy; add sour cream and cheeses.

• Butter a deep 9 x 13-inch baking dish. Layer half the noodles, beef mixture, and cheeses. Repeat layers.

• Bake covered at 325° for 30 minutes; remove covering and bake another 10 to 15 minutes.

PREP TIME: 20 MINUTES   COOKING TIME: 2 HOURS

Italian Manicotti

MAKES 6 SERVINGS

Manicotti is a little more trouble than some dishes, but it is well worth the effort, and leftovers freeze well.

1 pound lean ground round beef

3 cloves garlic, minced

2 onions, chopped

28-ounce can diced tomatoes, undrained

8-ounce package fresh mushrooms, sliced

1 teaspoon fennel seed

2 teaspoons basil

1 teaspoon seasoned salt

1/2 teaspoon pepper

2 10-ounce packages frozen chopped spinach, thawed and well drained

1/2 cup Parmesan cheese, divided

2 cups small curd cottage cheese, drained

1/4 teaspoon nutmeg

1/2 teaspoon pepper

14 manicotti shells

● In a large skillet, brown ground beef, then add garlic and onion, and reduce heat to low. Simmer for 10 minutes and drain. Add tomatoes and liquid, mushrooms, fennel seed, basil, salt, and pepper and stir to mix. Bring to a boil, reduce heat, and simmer for 10 minutes; stir occasionally.

● In a separate bowl, stir together spinach, half the Parmesan, cottage cheese, nutmeg, and pepper. In a greased 9 x 13-inch baking dish, spoon about one-third of beef sauce evenly over bottom of dish.

● Fill uncooked manicotti shells with spinach mixture and place on beef layer in baking dish. Repeat until all spinach mixture has been used in manicotti shells.

● Pour remaining beef sauce evenly over manicotti shells to cover. Sprinkle remaining Parmesan cheese over top. Cover and bake at 350° for 1 hour and 30 minutes or until shells are tender.

PREP TIME: 20 MINUTES   COOKING TIME: 55 MINUTES

Three-Cheese Fusilli Bake

MAKES 4 SERVINGS

If you don't have a soufflé dish, a deep, round casserole dish will work fine.

1 tablespoon salt
1 tablespoon olive oil
1 pound spinach fusilli
1 cup heavy cream
1/2 cup dry white wine
1/2 teaspoon Tabasco
1 1/2 cups blue cheese
1 cup brie cheese, rind removed, cubed
3 cups grated Cheddar cheese, divided
1 tablespoon dried thyme
2 tablespoons sage
1 to 2 tablespoons ground white pepper to taste
4 to 5 Roma tomatoes, peeled, thinly sliced
3 tablespoons grated Parmesan cheese
2 tablespoons snipped fresh basil

● Fill a large pot three-quarters full of water and bring to a boil. Add 1 tablespoon salt, 1 tablespoon oil, and fusilli, and cook until fusilli is al dente. Drain and rinse under cold water. Repeat draining process and set aside.

● In heavy saucepan, slowly heat to simmering the heavy cream, wine, and Tabasco, stirring constantly. Gradually add all cheeses, except 1 cup Cheddar and the Parmesan, a little at a time as they melt. Whisk or stir constantly as cheese melts and be sure not to let cream scorch or burn on bottom of saucepan.

● When cheeses have melted and mixture is smooth and creamy, whisk in thyme, sage, and white pepper. Remove from heat and continue stirring for 3 to 5 minutes as cheese mixture cools.

● In a greased 2 1/2-quart soufflé dish, arrange one-third of the cheese mixture over the fusilli and sprinkle with one-third of the remaining grated Cheddar cheese. Repeat process in two more layers, ending with grated Cheddar on top.

● Carefully put soufflé dish in oven and bake at 350° for 15 to 20 minutes. Remove from oven and cover with aluminum foil and bake another 15 minutes.

● Remove from oven and uncover. Place tomato slices over the top in nice overlapping design and sprinkle Parmesan on top. Bake at 350° for another 10 minutes uncovered. Remove from oven and sprinkle with fresh basil and serve.

PREP TIME: 20 MINUTES   COOKING TIME: 1 HOUR 55 MINUTES

Polenta Bake

MAKES 6 SERVINGS

Polenta is made from cornmeal and is a staple in northern Italy. It can be served as an appetizer or side dish, served hot with butter, or fried in squares.

Polenta

4 cups water

1 teaspoon salt

1 teaspoon pepper

1 cup polenta

Sauce

3 tablespoons oil

1 onion, minced

2 cloves garlic, minced

28-ounce can diced tomatoes and juice

1/4 cup tomato sauce

2 teaspoons dried oregano

2 bay leaves

1 teaspoon salt

1 teaspoon pepper

1/2 cup grated Asiago cheese

3/4 cup heavy cream

Fresh parsley sprigs

• In a medium saucepan, bring water to a boil and add salt, pepper, and polenta. Reduce heat, stirring occasionally, and cook for 40 to 45 minutes or until polenta separates from side of saucepan.

• In a prepared 10 x 15-inch baking dish, spread polenta evenly in bottom. Cover with plastic wrap and chill in refrigerator.

• In a heavy saucepan over moderate heat make sauce by heating oil, then sauté onion and garlic until they are translucent. Stir in diced tomatoes, tomato sauce, oregano, bay leaves, salt, and pepper. Cook about 20 to 25 minutes until sauce thickens to consistency of thin chowder.

• Remove from heat, retrieve bay leaves, and throw away. Pour sauce into a greased 10 x 15-inch baking dish and set aside.

• Remove polenta from refrigerator and cut into long strips, 2 to 3 inches wide. Lay strips of polenta in a criss cross pattern over sauce. Sprinkle with cheese and pour cream over top layer. Bake at 350° for 40 to 45 minutes. Remove from oven to cool for several minutes before serving. Cut into squares and serve. Garnish with fresh parsley.

Spinach-Baked Penne

MAKES 6 SERVINGS

This dish is easy to put together and extra easy to eat!

12- to 14-ounce package ground hot Italian sausage
4 cloves garlic, minced
2 onions, chopped
28-ounce can crushed tomatoes, undrained
1/2 cup pesto sauce
1/2 teaspoon salt
1/4 teaspoon pepper
10-ounce package penne or ziti
10-ounce package fresh spinach leaves, torn
2 cups shredded mozzarella cheese
1 cup freshly grated Parmesan cheese, divided

- In large skillet, brown sausage. Push sausage to one side in skillet, add garlic and onion, and cook a minute or two. Stir ingredients together, break apart sausage, and cook on low until sausage is no longer pink and cooked throughout.

- Drain sausage and pour in tomatoes and liquid. Cook on low for 10 minutes or until liquid begins to thicken into a sauce, stirring occasionally. Add pesto, salt, and pepper and stir to mix well.

- In large pot, add 2 to 3 times more water than penne or ziti and bring to a boil. Add pasta and cook until al dente. Drain pasta thoroughly and pour into a large bowl.

- Add spinach, mozzarella, and half the Parmesan to the pasta and stir to mix. Add tomato mixture and stir.

- Pour all ingredients into a greased 9 x 13-inch baking dish, spreading evenly. Sprinkle remaining Parmesan cheese over top of dish. Bake at 350° for 30 to 35 minutes or until bubbly.

PREP TIME: 15 MINUTES   COOKING TIME: 50 MINUTES

Vegetable Roast with Pasta

MAKES 6 SERVINGS

This delicious medley of vegetables and pasta is fit for a king!

3 tablespoons olive oil

2 tablespoons red wine vinegar

3 teaspoons Italian seasoning

1/2 teaspoon salt

1/2 teaspoon pepper

2 zucchini, cut in bite-size pieces

1/2 pound fresh mushrooms, halved

1 bunch green onions and tops, cut in 1-inch pieces

1 red bell pepper, seeded, cored and cut in bite-size pieces

1 green bell pepper, seeded, cored and cut in bite-size pieces

1/3 cup chopped fresh basil

10 ounces penne pasta

2 tomatoes, seeded and cut into bite-size pieces

8-ounce package shredded four-cheese blend

- In small ovenproof dish, mix together oil, vinegar, Italian seasoning, salt, and pepper. Set aside.

- Place zucchini, mushrooms, onion, and bell peppers in a greased 9 x 13-inch baking dish and sprinkle top with fresh basil. Drizzle oil and vinegar mixture over top and bake at 350° for 35 minutes.

- Fill a large pot with water and cook penne until al dente. Add tomatoes and pasta to vegetable mixture. Toss to coat, then sprinkle top with cheeses. Bake at 350° for 10 to 15 minutes until cheeses are melted.

Elegant Noodles

MAKES 4 TO 6 SERVINGS

Select plain noodles or any of the flavored noodles and pastas for a special way to serve up this tempting, tasty dish.

6 cups water

6 tablespoons chicken bouillon

8-ounce package fine egg noodles, divided

1 1/2 cups small curd cottage cheese

1 1/2 cups sour cream

1/2 teaspoon garlic powder

1/8 teaspoon white pepper

1/4 cup minced onion

2-ounce jar chopped pimientos, drained

1/4 teaspoon hot sauce

1 teaspoon Worcestershire sauce

12-ounce package shredded Cheddar cheese, divided

• In a large saucepan, combine water, chicken bouillon, and noodles; bring to a boil. Cook on low heat until all liquid is absorbed into the noodles, about 25 minutes.

• In a large bowl, combine cottage cheese, sour cream, garlic powder, pepper, onion, pimientos, hot sauce, and Worcestershire; mix well. Stir in the noodles.

• Place half the noodle mixture in a buttered 3-quart baking dish and top with half the shredded cheese. Add remaining noodle mixture and top with remaining cheese. Let marinate at room temperature for 2 hours.

• Bake covered at 325° for 1 hour. Remove cover and bake an additional 10 minutes.

Spinach-Rice Casserole

MAKES 4 SERVINGS

This casserole makes a great dish to serve with beef, pork, or chicken, and is a great "make ahead" dish.

10-ounce package frozen spinach, cooked and
  drained
3 cups cooked rice
8-ounce package shredded Cheddar cheese
2 tablespoons minced onion
5 eggs, beaten
1 cup milk
1/2 stick butter, melted
1 tablespoon Worcestershire sauce
1 teaspoon rosemary
1 teaspoon thyme
1/2 teaspoon marjoram
1 teaspoon salt

• Drain spinach thoroughly to remove all liquid. Mix together spinach, rice, cheese, and onion.

• In a separate bowl, combine eggs, milk, butter, Worcestershire sauce, and all seasonings. Add to spinach mixture and stir to mix.

• Pour into a greased 2-quart baking dish. Bake at 350° for 30 minutes or until heated thoroughly.

PREP TIME: 20 MINUTES   COOKING TIME: 25 MINUTES

Veggie Couscous

MAKES 4 TO 6 SERVINGS

For a change of pace, forget rice or potatoes and lighten up dinner with this delightful, colorful dish.

1/2 cup chopped crooked neck or yellow squash

1/2 cup chopped zucchini

1/2 bunch green onions with tops, chopped

1/4 cup chopped celery

1/4 cup chopped red bell pepper

2 cloves garlic, minced

3 tablespoons olive oil

14-ounce can garbanzos, drained

1/4 teaspoon cayenne

1/2 teaspoon cumin

1/2 teaspoon curry powder

1/2 teaspoon salt

1/4 teaspoon pepper

3 cups cooked couscous

3 tablespoons butter, melted

Fresh parsley or minced green onions

● Over low heat, sauté squash, zucchini, onions, celery, bell pepper, and garlic in oil until tender. Stir in garbanzos and seasonings and simmer to mix flavors for several minutes.

● Add couscous and stir to mix. Continue to simmer while stirring. Pour into a greased baking dish and drizzle butter over top. Bake at 350° for 15 minutes or until hot. Garnish with minced green onions or fresh parsley.

PREP TIME: 30 MINUTES   COOKING TIME: 20-25 MINUTES

Double Rice Casserole

MAKES 4 TO 6 SERVINGS

The pungent flavor of pine nuts is the perfect addition to plain rice. They are also a good addition to vegetables and salads.

3/4 cup pine nuts
3 tablespoons orange juice
1 cup dried currants
1 cup brown rice
1 cup wild rice
2 tablespoons grated orange zest
2 tablespoons snipped parsley
4 tablespoons olive oil
1 teaspoon salt
1/2 teaspoon pepper
1/3 cup grated Parmesan cheese
Fresh parsley

• Spread pine nuts on baking sheet and bake at 250° for 10 to 15 minutes, stirring once. Remove from oven and set aside. Pour orange juice over currants and set aside.

• Cook brown rice and wild rice according to package directions and mix together in separate bowl. To rice mixture, add pine nuts, currants, orange zest, parsley, olive oil, salt, and pepper. Mix thoroughly.

• Spoon mixture into a greased baking dish, cover with aluminum foil, and bake at 350° for 20 to 25 minutes until well heated. Sprinkle with Parmesan cheese and fresh parsley.

PREP TIME: 20 MINUTES   COOKING TIME: 40–45 MINUTES

Wild Rice with Hazelnuts

MAKES 4 TO 6 SERVINGS

The hazelnuts give a European touch to the wild rice. Not all grocery stores carry these nuts, so you may have to go to a gourmet shop to find them. However, the sweet, rich flavor is worth the extra effort.

1 cup hazelnuts, husked, chopped
1 cup wild rice, rinsed
4 cups chicken broth
1 cup white rice
1/4 teaspoon salt
1/4 teaspoon pepper
5 green onion tops, chopped
1 tablespoon butter

• Spread hazelnuts on baking sheet and toast in oven at 250° for 10 to 15 minutes. Remove from oven and set aside.

• Add wild rice to boiling chicken broth and stir. Reduce heat to simmer, cover, and cook 20 minutes. Stir in white rice, cover, and simmer about 20 to 25 minutes until liquid has been absorbed. Season with salt and pepper.

• Sauté green onions in butter until tender, stirring occasionally. Stir in hazelnuts just to warm, and pour into rice. Stir well and pour into a serving bowl.

PREP TIME: 20 MINUTES   COOKING TIME: 20–25 MINUTES

Herb Wild Rice Stuffing

MAKES 6 SERVINGS

Here's a new twist on a classic recipe. This stuffing will soon become a family favorite, and it can be served with chicken, turkey, pork, or beef.

3 to 4 tablespoons butter

1 cup chopped celery

1 cup chopped green onions and tops

2 cloves garlic, minced

3 tablespoons dry white wine

2 tablespoons maple syrup

1 teaspoon sage

1 teaspoon salt

1/2 teaspoon tarragon

1/2 teaspoon poultry seasoning

1/2 teaspoon thyme

3/4 cup cooked wild rice

8 cups plain, dry bread cubes

1/2 cup dried cranberries

1/2 to 1 cup chicken stock

3 tablespoons chopped fresh parsley

1/2 teaspoon black pepper

● In a large skillet, melt butter and sauté celery, onion, and garlic until onion is translucent. Add wine, bring to a boil, reduce heat, and simmer for several minutes.

● Stir in maple syrup, sage, salt, tarragon, poultry seasoning, and thyme, and mix well.

● In a separate bowl, combine wild rice, bread cubes, and cranberries; toss to mix well. Add onion mixture and stir. Slowly pour in a small amount of chicken stock and stir. Mixture should be moist and soupy; it will dry as it cooks. Stir in parsley and pepper.

● Pour into a greased baking dish and bake at 350° for 20 to 25 minutes or until heated throughout and golden brown on top.

Southwestern Risotto

MAKES 4 TO 6 SERVINGS

Here is a change of pace, and delicious too!

1/4 cup olive oil

1 bunch green onions and tops, chopped

1/2 cup chopped chopped celery

1/2 cup chopped red bell pepper

1/2 cup chopped green bell pepper

1/2 cup chopped yellow bell pepper

1 1/2 cups uncooked Arborio rice

1/2 cup tequila

2 cups chicken broth

16-ounce package frozen whole kernel corn, thawed

8-ounce package cream cheese, cubed

● In a large skillet, heat oil and sauté onion, celery, and bell peppers until vegetables are tender. Push vegetables to outside edges of skillet, turn up heat, and add rice to the center.

● Toast the rice, toss, and stir until rice grains look translucent. Add tequila and cook until tequila has been absorbed. Pour chicken broth into rice and cook until liquid is absorbed. Stir in the corn.

● Drop a few cubes of cream cheese in rice, stir as cheese melts and combines with rice. Continue to add remaining cream cheese, coating all rice with melted cheese.

● Serve immediately or pour into a sprayed casserole dish, cool and refrigerate. To serve, reheat at 350° for 15 to 20 minutes or until heated throughout.

Vegetable Sides & Main Dishes

Cheesy Asparagus

Broccoli-Corn Casserole

Broccoli-Rice Bake

Broccoli Casserole Amandine

Broccoli-Mushroom Bake

Cheese Broccoli

Easy Carrot Casserole

Southern Carrot-Pecan Casserole

Corn Casserole

Cheesy Cauliflower Casserole

Crowned Artichokes

Corn Pudding Casserole

Unusual Cabbage Casserole

Harvest Corn Casserole

Green Chili Casserole

Eggplant Special

Eggplant-Tomato Festival

Bean & Bacon Casserole

Cowboy Casserole

Lima Bean Special

Baked Bean Special

Squash & Tomato Bake

Stuffed Yellow Peppers

New Potatoes & Sweet Potatoes

Mushroom & Potato One-Dish

Mashed Potatoes with Arugula

Potatoes with Gruyère

Mashed Potato Casserole

Sweet Potato Soufflé

Scalloped Potatoes

Sweet Potato One-Dish

Spinach & Artichoke Bake

Spinach Special

Zucchini with Goat Cheese

Creamed Spinach Casserole

Zucchini Bake

Zucchini, Squash & Tomato Casserole

Stuffed Squash

Summer Squash Casserole

Spinach & Cheese Bake

Vegetable Roast

Vegetable Bake

Vegetable Casserole

Tomato & Zucchini Pie

Braised Onion with Celery

Ratatouille with Feta Cheese

Chili-Stuffed Chayote Squash

Winter Vegetable Stew with Cheddar and Croutons

Black Bean & Corn Chili

Braised Winter Root Vegetables

Cheesy Asparagus

MAKES 4 SERVINGS

Asparagus is often reserved as a special, company dish, but your family will ask for this casserole on a regular basis.

2 15-ounce cans asparagus spears, liquid reserved
1/2 stick butter
5 tablespoons flour
Salt and pepper to taste
1/2 cup milk
1/2 teaspoon Worcestershire sauce
Dash cayenne pepper
4 eggs, boiled, sliced
1/4 pound Cheddar cheese, cubed
1/2 cup almonds, sliced
1 cup crushed Ritz cracker crumbs

● Reserve 3/4 cup asparagus liquid and set asparagus aside. In saucepan melt the butter and gradually blend in flour until smooth, adding salt and pepper. Slowly add asparagus liquid and milk, stirring until thickened and smooth. You may add more milk if liquid is too thick. Add Worcestershire sauce and cayenne pepper.

● Layer the casserole in a lightly greased 8 x 11-inch baking pan as follows: asparagus, eggs, cheese, and almonds, and repeat layers. Spoon sauce over layers. Sprinkle cracker crumbs over casserole and bake at 350° for 20 to 25 minutes.

PREP TIME: 20 MINUTES   COOKING TIME: 25 MINUTES

Broccoli-Corn Casserole

MAKES 6 SERVINGS

Everybody loves broccoli and corn, but when you add seasoned stuffing, butter, and cheese, you get quite a combination. The family will love it, and guests will be asking for the recipe.

16-ounce package frozen chopped broccoli
10-ounce package frozen cream-style corn
10¹/2-ounce can cream of mushroom soup
1 egg, beaten
1¹/2 cups herb-seasoned stuffing mix, divided
¹/2 stick butter, melted
1 onion, chopped
²/3 cup grated Cheddar cheese

● Prepare broccoli and corn as package directs. Combine broccoli, corn, soup, egg, half the stuffing mix, butter, and onion. Pour into a greased 1¹/2-quart baking dish.

● Sprinkle remaining stuffing mix over mixture, then sprinkle cheese. Bake at 350° for 25 to 30 minutes or until heated.

PREP TIME: 10 MINUTES   COOKING TIME: 40 MINUTES

Broccoli-Rice Bake

MAKES 6 SERVINGS

This is a wonderful dish to "make ahead." You'll have a vegetable and a side dish rolled up into one!

10-ounce package frozen broccoli florets

1 onion, chopped

2 tablespoons butter

10½-ounce can cream of chicken soup

10½-ounce can cream of celery soup

½ cup milk

8-ounce package mild Mexican Velveeta cheese, cubed

3 cups instant rice, cooked

• Cook broccoli; drain. In a large skillet, sauté onion in the butter. Add soups, milk, cheese, and rice. Heat on low just until cheese has melted.

• Pour into a 9 x 13-inch casserole dish greased with nonstick vegetable spray. Cover and bake at 350° for 25 to 30 minutes.

Broccoli Casserole Amandine

MAKES 4 SERVINGS

Former President Bush (the Senior) is the only person in the world who doesn't like broccoli, which everyone knows is really healthy (but don't tell the kids!).

2 10-ounce packages frozen chopped broccoli

3 tablespoons butter

2 tablespoons flour

2 cups milk

3/4 cup grated Parmesan cheese

1 teaspoon salt

1/4 teaspoon ground pepper

1/4 pound mushrooms, sliced

1/2 cup chopped almonds

4 slices cooked bacon, crumbled

1/2 cup buttered bread crumbs

Dash paprika

• Cook broccoli according to package directions; drain.

• In a saucepan, melt butter and blend in flour. Add milk slowly and cook until thick, stirring constantly. Add cheese and stir until melted. Season with salt and pepper and add mushrooms.

• Remove from heat and pour sauce into a 2-quart baking dish coated with cooking spray. Add broccoli. Put almonds and bacon on top of the broccoli and sprinkle with bread crumbs and paprika. Bake at 350° for 20 minutes.

PREP TIME: 15 MINUTES   COOKING TIME: 40 MINUTES

Broccoli-Mushroom Bake

MAKES 8 SERVINGS

Fresh mushrooms add a special touch to broccoli. Cooked together with cheese and eggs, you have a real winner!

4 slices buttered bread

2 16-ounce packages frozen broccoli spears

1/2 to 3/4 pound mushrooms, sliced

4 tablespoons chopped onion

2 to 4 tablespoons butter

3/4 cup grated Cheddar cheese

1 1/2 cups small curd cottage cheese, drained

2 eggs, beaten

1 teaspoon Worcestershire sauce

1 teaspoon salt

1/2 teaspoon pepper

• Cut bread into small cubes to make croutons. Toast in oven at 250° for 15 minutes or until crisp. Set aside.

• Cook broccoli according to package directions, drain, and place in a greased baking dish. In skillet, sauté mushrooms and onion in butter until tender and translucent. Transfer mixture to baking dish with broccoli.

• Mix together Cheddar cheese, cottage cheese, eggs, Worcestershire sauce, salt, and pepper. Pour over broccoli and drop croutons on top. Bake at 350° for 20 to 25 minutes.

Cheese Broccoli

PREP TIME: 5 MINUTES   COOKING TIME: 35 MINUTES

MAKES 6 SERVINGS

Healthful eating is a snap with this easy, speedy broccoli dish.

2 10-ounce packages frozen chopped broccoli, thawed
10 1/2-ounce can cream of mushroom soup
1/2 cup mayonnaise
1 cup grated Cheddar cheese
1 onion, chopped
1 cup chopped celery
8 Ritz crackers, crushed
1/2 stick butter

• Mix together broccoli, mushroom soup, mayonnaise, cheese, onion, and celery. Pour into a greased baking dish and top with crushed crackers.

• Cut butter into thin slices and place on top of crackers. Bake uncovered at 350° for 35 minutes.

Easy Carrot Casserole

PREP TIME: 15 MINUTES   COOKING TIME: 1 HOUR

MAKES 4 SERVINGS

Here's the perfect recipe to showcase the natural sweetness and bright color of carrots.

2 cups cooked, mashed carrots
1 cup milk
3 eggs, beaten
1/2 stick butter, melted
1 cup chopped pecans
1/2 cup sugar
1 teaspoon salt
1 teaspoon baking powder
2 tablespoons flour
1/4 teaspoon cinnamon

• Combine carrots, milk, eggs, butter, and pecans. In a separate bowl, mix together sugar, salt, baking powder, flour, and cinnamon, and slowly add to carrots.

• Mix thoroughly and pour into 2-quart casserole prepared with cooking spray. Bake at 350° for 1 hour.

PREP TIME: 20 MINUTES   COOKING TIME: 1 HOUR

Southern Carrot-Pecan Casserole

MAKES 8 SERVINGS

This is not your average carrot casserole. This dish could easily be put in the gourmet category for the discriminating palate.

3 *pounds carrots, peeled and sliced*

2/3 *cup chopped pecans*

4 *tablespoons butter, softened*

2/3 *cup sugar*

1/4 *cup milk*

2 *eggs, slightly beaten*

3 *tablespoons flour*

1 1/4 *teaspoons vanilla extract*

1 1/2 *tablespoons grated orange rind*

1/4 *teaspoon ground nutmeg*

● In a saucepan, cover carrots with water and boil 15 to 20 minutes, just until tender. Spread pecans on baking sheet in one layer. Bake at 250° for 10 to 15 minutes, stirring once or twice. Remove from oven to cool.

● Drain carrots and mash. Blend in butter, sugar, pecans, and remaining ingredients until thoroughly mixed. Spoon into a lightly greased, 8-inch baking dish. Bake at 350° for 45 minutes.

Corn Casserole

MAKES 8 SERVINGS

Everybody loves corn, and this quick and easy casserole is a great crowd pleaser. Adjust the hot sauce to suit your family's palette.

15-ounce can cream-style corn
15-ounce can whole kernel corn, drained
8-ounce package shredded cheese
1 green bell pepper, chopped
1 onion, chopped
2 eggs, beaten
4-ounce jar chopped pimientos, drained
1/4 teaspoon salt
1/4 teaspoon pepper
1/2 to 1 teaspoon hot sauce
1 cup cracker crumbs

• Mix together all ingredients and spoon into a lightly greased baking dish. Bake at 350° for 45 minutes to 1 hour.

Cheesy Cauliflower Casserole

MAKES 4 SERVINGS

The creamy, cheesy cauliflower featured in this casserole is a great way to get the kids to eat cauliflower.

1 head cauliflower
3/4 teaspoon salt
1 cup sour cream
1 1/2 cups shredded Cheddar cheese, divided
1/4 teaspoon white pepper

• Remove any brown spots from cauliflower and break into smaller pieces. Place cauliflower in saucepan. Cover with water and add 1/4 teaspoon salt and boil until slightly tender.

• Drain thoroughly and put half the cauliflower into a lightly greased 1-quart baking dish. In a separate bowl, mix together sour cream, half the cheese, remaining salt, and white pepper.

• Pour half the cheese mixture over the cauliflower, add remaining cauliflower, then add remaining cheese mixture. Top with remaining 3/4 cup cheese. Bake at 350° for 10 to15 minutes or until heated throughout.

PREP TIME: 15 MINUTES   COOKING TIME: 25 MINUTES

Crowned Artichokes

MAKES 8 SERVINGS

The artichoke was prized by Ancient Romans as the food of the nobility. Share this noble treat with your loved ones.

6 to 8 cans artichoke bottoms, drained

1 large clove garlic

4 tablespoons minced green onion

2 tablespoons butter

10-ounce package frozen chopped spinach, cooked, drained

3 tablespoons sour cream

3 tablespoons mayonnaise

1/2 teaspoon salt

4 ounces Boubel cheese

● Rub artichokes with garlic and place in a greased baking dish. Finely mince garlic and sprinkle a small amount on artichoke bottoms. In a skillet sauté onion in butter until tender.

● Roll cooked spinach in paper towels to drain thoroughly. Add spinach, sour cream, mayonnaise, and salt. Pour mixture over artichoke bottoms.

● Cut cheese into 10 thin slices and then cut each slice into 3 to 4 strips. Lay strips over spinach and criss cross in a lattice design. Bake at 350° for 20 minutes or until cheese melts. Cut into small squares and let stand 5 minutes before serving.

PREP TIME: 15 MINUTES   COOKING TIME: 1 HOUR

Corn Pudding Casserole

MAKES 4 SERVINGS

It's hard to resist having corn on the menu at least once a week, but fresh corn is the best!

6 thick slices bacon

1 cup chopped leeks

1/4 cup diced red bell pepper

1/4 cup diced green bell pepper

3 large ears fresh corn

3 egg yolks

2 cups heavy cream

1/2 teaspoon dry mustard

1/4 teaspoon Worcestershire sauce

1/4 teaspoon Tabasco

Salt to taste

1/2 teaspoon ground black pepper

1 tablespoon snipped fresh parsley

● In a skillet, fry bacon until crisp. Drain on paper towels to cool. Add leeks and bell peppers to skillet and sauté over medium heat until tender. Remove from skillet with slotted spoon to drain and place in a mixing bowl. Set aside.

● Heat large pot with water to boiling and carefully drop ears of corn into water. Cook for 5 to 6 minutes until tender. Remove from pot and rinse under cold water to cool.

● When corn has cooled, cut kernels from cob and add to mixing bowl with leeks and bell peppers. Crumble cooled bacon and add to mixing bowl. Mix well and sprinkle over bottom of a 4 x 6-inch greased baking dish.

● In a separate bowl, whisk together egg yolks, heavy cream, mustard, Worcestershire sauce, Tabasco, salt, pepper, and parsley. Slowly pour into baking dish and bake at 350° for 40 to 45 minutes. Garnish with fresh parsley.

PREP TIME: 15 MINUTES   COOKING TIME: 30 MINUTES

Unusual Cabbage Casserole

MAKES 6 SERVINGS

The best way to a delicious cabbage casserole is to pick the right head of cabbage. The cabbage should have fresh, crisp-looking leaves that are firmly packed and should be heavy for its size. With a cream sauce and cheese, you have a "cabbage special."

6 cups shredded cabbage

3 tablespoons plus 1 teaspoon butter or margarine

3 tablespoons flour

2 cups milk

4-ounce can sliced mushrooms, drained

1/2 teaspoon salt

1/4 teaspoon pepper

1 cup grated sharp Cheddar cheese

- Place shredded cabbage in a large Dutch oven. Add boiling water, cover, and boil 5 minutes. Drain. Place cabbage in a large, lightly greased baking dish.

- In a large skillet, melt 3 tablespoons butter and whisk in flour. Cook over low heat until well blended. Gradually add milk, stirring until thick and smooth. In a small saucepan, sauté drained mushrooms in 1 teaspoon butter. Add to white sauce. Season with salt and pepper.

- Pour white sauce over cabbage and top with grated cheese. Bake at 350° for 30 minutes or until cheese melts and sauce is bubbly.

PREP TIME: 20 MINUTES   COOKING TIME: 1 HOUR 10 MINUTES

Harvest Corn Casserole

MAKES 4 SERVINGS

This hearty, colorful casserole may become your new favorite side dish. Make it for your next pot luck contribution or when you feel the need for some real comfort food.

Salt and pepper

6 to 8 ears corn, cleaned

8-ounce package cream cheese or goat cheese

4 to 6 tablespoons butter

1/4 cup flour

4 1/2-ounce can diced green chilies, drained

2 1/4 cups milk

Dash cayenne pepper

Dash salt

4 eggs, slightly beaten

● Salt and pepper ears of corn and brown in large buttered skillet. Cut kernels and pulp from ears and return to skillet. Mix cheese and butter and add to skillet to melt. Stir flour in melted butter and mix thoroughly.

● In separate bowl, mix green chilies, milk, cayenne pepper, and salt and stir in eggs. Pour into skillet and mix with corn. Pour entire mixture into a lightly greased 7 x 11-inch baking dish.

● Bake covered at 350° for 1 hour or until center is firm and edges are brown.

PREP TIME: 20 MINUTES   COOKING TIME: 1 HOUR 30 MINUTES

Green Chili Casserole

MAKES 4 SERVINGS

Here's a great casserole to go with Mexican food or to perk up a ho-hum meal.

1 cup half-and-half
2 eggs
1/3 cup flour
3 4-ounce cans whole green chilies or 1 3-ounce can jalapeño peppers
8 ounces grated Monterey Jack Cheese
8 ounces grated Cheddar cheese
8-ounce can tomato sauce

• Mix half-and-half, eggs, and flour until smooth. Cut chilies or peppers down the middle, rinse out seeds, and drain chilies on paper towels.

• Mix cheeses and set aside a little for topping. In a lightly greased 1¹/2-quart baking dish, make layers of chilies, remaining cheese, and egg mixture.

• Pour tomato sauce over top and sprinkle with remaining cheese. Bake at 350° for 1¹/2 hours or until cooked in center.

PREP TIME: 15 MINUTES   COOKING TIME: 40 MINUTES

Eggplant Special

MAKES 6 SERVINGS

Eggplants and tomatoes just go together. And with croutons and cheese, you have a winner.

2 large eggplants
2 15-ounce cans diced tomatoes, liquid reserved
1 egg, beaten
1/4 cup salsa
1 cup seasoned croutons
8-ounce package shredded Cheddar cheese

• Peel eggplants, slice, and cook in boiling water until tender. Place in a lightly greased 9 x 13-inch baking dish.

• Drain tomatoes, reserving liquid. Pour tomatoes over eggplant. Whisk together egg, reserved liquid, and salsa, then pour over eggplant mixture.

• Sprinkle croutons and cheese over top. Bake at 350° for 40 to 45 minutes.

PREP TIME: 15 MINUTES   COOKING TIME: 40 MINUTES

Eggplant-Tomato Festival

MAKES 4 SERVINGS

A little known fact: the eggplant is not a vegetable; it's actually a fruit that is related to the potato and tomato. For best flavor, choose an eggplant that is smooth-skinned and heavy for its size, and avoid those with soft or brown spots.

1 large eggplant
Vegetable oil
1 large onion, sliced
1 large green bell pepper, sliced
2 teaspoons salt
1 teaspoon white pepper
3/4 teaspoon basil
4 to 5 tomatoes, sliced
3/4 cup bread crumbs
3/4 cup grated Cheddar cheese

● Cut eggplant into 1/4-inch thick slices. Sauté in vegetable oil, drain, and set aside. Sauté onions and peppers in oil and drain.

● In a greased 2-quart baking dish, place a layer of eggplant slices and season with salt, pepper, and basil. Repeat with layers of onion and bell pepper, and remaining eggplant, seasoning after each layer.

● Place tomato slices over eggplant and sprinkle bread crumbs and cheese over tomatoes. Bake at 350° for 30 to 40 minutes or until browned on top.

PREP TIME: 20 MINUTES   COOKING TIME: 1 HOUR 15 MINUTES

Bean & Bacon Casserole

MAKES 8 SERVINGS

This is a twist on regular baked beans. Each bean complements the other. Try it, you'll like it!

1 pound bacon

1/4 cup cider vinegar

3/4 cup ketchup

1 cup packed brown sugar

3 red onions, chopped

1/4 teaspoon dry mustard

1/4 teaspoon salt

2 15-ounce cans baby lima beans, drained

15-ounce can red kidney beans, drained

16-ounce can pork and beans

- Fry bacon and drain, reserving enough bacon grease to cover bottom of skillet. In same skillet, add vinegar, ketchup, brown sugar, onions, dry mustard, and salt.

- Simmer until onion is tender and brown sugar has dissolved. Pour mixture into a lightly greased 3-quart baking dish and add all the beans. Stir to mix and top with bacon.

- Cover and bake at 350° for 1 hour. Remove cover and cook another 15 minutes.

Cowboy Casserole

MAKES 6 SERVINGS

This "cowboy" has been to Old Mexico and has a taste for the spiced-up tortilla.

1 tablespoon olive oil

10 corn tortillas

2 14¹/2-ounce cans Mexican stewed tomatoes

¹/4 teaspoon cumin

4¹/2-ounce can green chilies, drained

³/4 cup chopped onion

1 green bell pepper, chopped

15-ounce can black beans, drained

1 cup loosely packed fresh cilantro, chopped

¹/4 teaspoon chili powder

2 cups grated sharp Cheddar cheese

● Pour olive oil into large baking dish. Place four corn tortillas in the bottom of the dish. Cut the remaining tortillas into strips and set aside.

● Layer the tomatoes, cumin, chilies, onion, bell pepper, beans, cilantro, and chili powder in the baking dish on top of the tortillas. Top with the strips of tortillas and the grated Cheddar cheese. Cover casserole with foil and bake at 400° for 20 minutes.

PREP TIME: 20 MINUTES   COOKING TIME: 1 HOUR

Lima Bean Special

MAKES 4 SERVINGS

Lima beans are often overlooked in the kitchen, but with this recipe, no one will forget the limas!

2 cups water

4 cups fresh, shelled baby lima beans or
    frozen baby lima beans

5 slices bacon

2 1/2 tablespoons flour

3 tablespoons brown sugar

1 1/2 teaspoons salt

1/4 teaspoon pepper

1 1/2 tablespoons dry mustard

1 1/2 tablespoons lemon juice

3/4 cup dry bread crumbs

3 tablespoons butter, melted

1/2 to 3/4 cup shredded sharp Cheddar cheese

• Lightly grease an 8-inch baking dish. In saucepan, bring water to boil and add lima beans. Return to boil, then reduce heat and simmer until tender, approximately 20 minutes. Drain and reserve one cup of liquid.

• Place lima beans in baking dish. Set aside. Cook bacon until crisp. Drain, crumble, and set aside. Save 2 tablespoons of bacon drippings in skillet. Add flour and stir over low heat until smooth. Cook one additional minute and gradually add reserved bean liquid.

• Continue to cook over low heat, stirring constantly, until thickened. Stir in brown sugar, salt, pepper, mustard, and lemon juice. Pour mixture over lima beans. Combine bread crumbs and melted butter and sprinkle over lima beans.

• Bake at 350° for 25 minutes. Sprinkle top of casserole with shredded cheese and bake an additional 8 to 10 minutes. Sprinkle top with crumbled bacon.

Baked Bean Special

MAKES 12 SERVINGS

Everyone knows that baked beans are a must for outdoor cookouts, but they're also perfect to accompany a smoked brisket and ideal for just plain family fare.

$1^1/_2$ *pounds ground chuck or ground round beef*

1 tablespoon seasoning salt

1 teaspoon pepper

1 cup chopped onion

1 bell pepper, seeded, chopped

$^2/_3$ *cup barbecue sauce*

$^1/_4$ *cup molasses*

1 cup packed brown sugar

2 16-ounce cans pork and beans

2 16-ounce cans ranch-style beans

2 16-ounce cans baked beans

● Season ground meat with seasoning salt and pepper and sauté until brown and crumbly. Drain thoroughly. Add onion and bell pepper and cook until tender.

● Pour in barbecue sauce, molasses, and brown sugar, and stir to mix. Add beans and stir well. Spoon into a lightly greased 9 x 13-inch baking dish and bake at 350° for 30 to 40 minutes, or until bubbly and heated throughout.

PREP TIME: 20 MINUTES   COOKING TIME: 40 MINUTES

Squash & Tomato Bake

MAKES 4 SERVINGS

You can't beat this combination of squash, tomato, and mozzarella cheese.

1 pound zucchini, sliced

1 pound yellow squash, sliced

2 15-ounce cans Italian stewed tomatoes

2 teaspoons sugar

2 tablespoons flour

1 teaspoon paprika

1 teaspoon salt

1/4 teaspoon white pepper

1/2 teaspoon basil

1/4 teaspoon garlic powder

2 cups shredded mozzarella cheese, divided

1/3 cup grated Parmesan cheese

• Cook zucchini and squash almost covered in water in a saucepan. Bring water to a boil, reduce heat, and simmer for 5 to 10 minutes, stirring several times, until squash is fork tender. Drain and set aside.

• In a saucepan, pour tomatoes with a 1/2 cup of their liquid and mix with sugar, flour, paprika, salt, pepper, basil, and garlic powder. Heat for 5 to 10 minutes, stirring several times, and remove from heat.

• In a lightly greased 2-quart baking dish, layer half the squash, one-third of the tomato mixture, half the mozzarella, and one-third of the tomato mixture.

• Repeat layers with remaining squash, tomato mixture, and mozzarella. Bake at 350° for 20 to 25 minutes. Remove from oven, sprinkle Parmesan over top, and return to brown for 5 minutes. Let stand for 10 minutes before serving.

PREP TIME: 20 MINUTES   COOKING TIME: 50 MINUTES

Stuffed Yellow Peppers

MAKES 4 SERVINGS

Yellow peppers bring a lovely color and unique flavor to any dish. When stuffed, they bring a change of pace to any meal.

4 large yellow bell peppers
1 cup instant long-grain rice
3 tablespoons dried currants
1/3 cup orange juice
2 tablespoons olive oil
1/2 cup chopped celery
1/2 cup chopped green onions with tops
2 cloves garlic, minced
3 tablespoons chopped sun-dried tomatoes
2 tablespoons minced fresh basil
2 tablespoons snipped parsley
1 teaspoon ground coriander
1/2 teaspoon salt
1/4 teaspoon white pepper
Paprika

● Trim stem tops from bell peppers and reserve. Carefully remove membranes and seeds without tearing or splitting outside of peppers. Wash, drain, and set aside.

● Cook rice according to package directions and set aside. Soak currants in orange juice and set aside. In a skillet, heat oil and sauté celery, onions, and garlic until tender, stirring occasionally.

● While celery-onion mixture is simmering, remove currants from orange juice and drain. Add currants, sun-dried tomatoes, basil, parsley, coriander, salt, and pepper and stir to mix. Stir in rice and mix all ingredients thoroughly. Spoon rice filling into each pepper and replace stem tops.

● Arrange peppers next to each other in a lightly greased baking dish. Cover dish and bake at 350° for 30 to 35 minutes or until outside of peppers are tender. Remove from oven, uncover, and sprinkle lightly with paprika. Return to oven and bake an additional 10 to 15 minutes until tops are lightly browned.

PREP TIME: 30 MINUTES   COOKING TIME: 45 MINUTES

New Potatoes &
Sweet Potatoes

MAKES 6 SERVINGS

This makes an attractive dish, because the sweet pota-toes add color and a distinct flavor contrast for pota-toes that are a little different.

1 pound sweet potatoes, peeled and quartered
1 pound large new potatoes, peeled and quartered
1 1/4 teaspoons salt, divided
1 teaspoon white pepper, divided
1/4 teaspoon nutmeg, divided
1 bunch green onions, chopped, divided
1/2 cup sour cream
1/2 cup heavy cream, whipped
1/2 cup bread crumbs or croutons
3 tablespoons butter, melted
1/4 cup green onion tops, minced

• Cover sweet potatoes with water in saucepan and cook until tender. In separate saucepan, cook new potatoes, covered in water, until tender. Allow both to cool, and mash in separate bowl.

• Sprinkle half the salt, pepper, nutmeg, and green onions into the sweet potatoes, and the remaining half into the new potatoes. Stir to mix.

• Gently fold sour cream into whipped cream and stir to mix. Spoon half the whipped cream mixture into the sweet potatoes, and the remaining half into the new potatoes.

• In a lightly greased 2-quart soufflé dish, layer half the sweet potatoes, and half the new potatoes and repeat layers. Swirl a knife once throughout the dish, then sprinkle with bread crumbs on top.

• Drizzle melted butter on top and garnish with minced green onion tops. Bake at 350° for 30 minutes or until golden brown on top.

Mushroom & Potato One-Dish

MAKES 6 TO 8 SERVINGS

Portobello and shiitake mushrooms make the lowly potato stand out in this casserole.

6 *potatoes*

Salt

1/2 stick butter, divided

8 ounces portobello mushrooms, sliced

8 ounces shiitake mushrooms, stemmed, sliced

1/2 teaspoon seasoned salt

1/4 teaspoon white pepper

1/4 cup chopped chives

1/3 cup grated Parmesan cheese

1/4 cup olive oil

- Wash and peel potatoes, then cut in 1/8-inch slices. In a large saucepan, with a little salt, bring water to boil, and blanch potatoes for 3 minutes. Drain and pat slices dry with paper towels.

- Melt half the butter in a skillet. Sauté the portobello mushrooms until tender. Remove mushrooms to a bowl. With remaining butter, sauté the shiitake mushrooms. Add the portobello mushrooms and cook. Add seasoned salt and pepper and stir in the chives.

- In a buttered 3-quart baking dish, layer one-fourth of the potatoes in an overlapping spiral. Top with one third of the mushrooms and sprinkle with 2 tablespoons of the Parmesan cheese. Drizzle with 1 or 2 tablespoons of olive oil.

- Repeat layer twice, ending with potato slices and drizzling with remaining oil. Cover and bake at 375° for 1 hour or until potatoes are tender. After the hour cooking time, remove cover and brown potatoes. Let stand 5 to 10 minutes before serving.

PREP TIME: 15 MINUTES   COOKING TIME: 45 MINUTES

Mashed Potatoes with Arugula

MAKES 6 SERVINGS

Try a different taste for a mashed potato favorite.

3 to 4 cloves garlic

1/4 cup olive oil, divided

Salt

White pepper

3 pounds baking potatoes

2 14-ounce cans chicken broth

2 bunches arugula, washed

4 tablespoons butter, divided

2 cups milk, divided

Fresh parsley, or fresh green onions with tops

Paprika

• Place garlic cloves on aluminum foil. Coat with small amount of olive oil and sprinkle with salt and pepper. Loosely close foil. Place in a small baking dish and bake at 350° for 30 to 40 minutes until garlic is soft. Remove from oven to cool. Set aside.

• Wash potatoes thoroughly and peel. (It's acceptable to leave peel on the potatoes and many people prefer them with peels.) Cut into large chunks and place in a large saucepan. Add chicken broth to saucepan. Add just enough water to cover potatoes. Bring broth to boil, reduce heat slightly, and cook for 25 to 30 minutes until potatoes are soft.

• Meanwhile, wash arugula thoroughly to remove all grit in leaves. Hold bottom of arugula with tongs and dip the leaves into boiling broth of potatoes. Drain on absorbent towels, pull leaves apart, and pat dry. Snip larger leaves into smaller pieces and set aside.

• When potatoes are soft enough to mash, drain and remove from saucepan. Empty liquid from pan and return pan to heat for a few seconds just until all liquid evaporates.

• Remove from heat and add potatoes. Mash with potato masher until all lumps are gone. Squeeze roasted garlic from outer skins and mash on separate plate. Add garlic and half the butter to potatoes and stir to mix. Continue mashing to remove any lumps.

• Slowly pour milk into potatoes, stirring constantly. Use the amount of milk necessary for the desired consistency of mashed potatoes: more milk for creamier potatoes, less milk for drier potatoes.

• Drizzle potatoes with olive oil and add salt and white pepper generously. Add half the arugula and taste. Adjust salt, pepper, and butter and add more arugula to taste. Garnish with any remaining arugula and parsley or green onions with tops. Sprinkle with paprika, if desired.

PREP TIME: 20 MINUTES   COOKING TIME: 1 HOUR 50 MINUTES

Potatoes with Gruyère

MAKES 6 SERVINGS

The mild and delicious cheese used in this recipe gives the potatoes a real boost.

3 pounds potatoes, peeled and quartered

1 teaspoon salt

1/4 teaspoon black pepper

1/4 teaspoon nutmeg

2 cups shredded Gruyère cheese

14-ounce can chicken broth

4 tablespoons butter

• Preheat oven to 450°. Lightly grease a large baking dish. Slice potatoes paper thin and transfer to a large bowl. Sprinkle with salt, pepper, and nutmeg and stir gently. In the baking dish, make three layers of potatoes topped with cheese, then pour chicken broth over all layers. Dot with butter on top.

• Bake covered for 20 minutes, then reduce temperature to 350° and bake for about 1 1/2 hours or until top is golden brown.

PREP TIME: 15 MINUTES   COOKING TIME: 1 HOUR

Mashed Potato Casserole

MAKES 6 SERVINGS

Mashed potatoes may be made in many different ways and this tasty treat is no disappointment.

1 onion, quartered

1 cup grated Cheddar cheese

1/4 cup butter, melted

1/2 cup milk

3 eggs

2 teaspoons salt

1/4 teaspoon pepper

1/4 cup snipped fresh parsley

3 potatoes, peeled and quartered

• Preheat oven to 350°. In a food processor, add onion, cheese, and butter, and chop finely. Add milk, eggs, salt, pepper, and parsley; blend. Add potatoes, one at a time, and continue to blend thoroughly.

• Pour into a lightly greased 1 1/2-quart casserole. Bake covered at 350° for 1 hour.

PREP TIME: 20 MINUTES   COOKING TIME: 45 MINUTES

Sweet Potato Soufflé

MAKES 6 SERVINGS

If a soufflé dish is not in your cabinets, just use a deep casserole dish. The cinnamon and brown sugar give it the magic touch, while the egg whites impart the light and fluffy texture.

5 cups canned sweet potatoes, drained, chopped
1 teaspoon cinnamon
1 cup applesauce
1 teaspoon vanilla
1 egg yolk
2 egg whites
2 tablespoons butter, melted
2/3 cup packed brown sugar
2 tablespoons flour

• Process or blend sweet potatoes, cinnamon, and applesauce until smooth. Fold in vanilla and egg yolk and mix thoroughly.

• Beat egg whites to form stiff peaks. Gently fold egg whites into potato mixture and slowly scoop into a lightly greased 1 1/2-quart soufflé dish (or a 2-quart casserole dish).

• In a separate bowl, mix butter, brown sugar, and flour. Sprinkle over sweet potatoes and bake at 350° for 35 to 45 minutes or until set.

PREP TIME: 10 MINUTES   COOKING TIME: 1 HOUR 35 MINUTES

Scalloped Potatoes

MAKES 6 SERVINGS

Scalloped most often refers to layers with a cream or cheese sauce between the layers. With this dish, the cook puts all the "good stuff" on the potatoes for you.

1 cup milk

1/2 cup heavy cream

12/3 cups grated extra-sharp Cheddar cheese

1 cup shredded Monterey Jack cheese

1/4 cup ketchup

2 teaspoons Worcestershire sauce

1/4 teaspoon black pepper

1/2 teaspoon salt

21/2 pounds peeled Idaho potatoes, cut into
   1/4-inch-thick slices

2 cups sliced onion

2 tablespoons snipped fresh parsley

• In a medium bowl, combine milk, cream, 3/4 cup Cheddar cheese, 1/2 cup Monterey Jack cheese, ketchup, Worcestershire, pepper, and salt. Stir well and set aside.

• Lightly grease a 9 x 13-inch baking dish with cooking spray. Arrange half the potatoes and half the onion in the bottom of the baking dish. Spoon half the milk mixture over the potatoes. Repeat layers; top with remaining cheeses and parsley.

• Cover and bake at 350° for 1 hour 15 minutes. Uncover; bake an additional 20 minutes or until potatoes are tender and cheese is browned.

Sweet Potato One-Dish

MAKES 4 SERVINGS

The sweet potato is the perfect dish in the fall. It wouldn't be Thanksgiving without this bountiful and elegant casserole.

3 cups cooked, mashed sweet potatoes

3/4 cup sugar

1/2 teaspoon salt

3 tablespoons butter, softened

2 eggs

1/2 cup milk

1 teaspoon vanilla

1 cup packed brown sugar

1/3 cup plain flour

1 cup chopped pecans

3 tablespoons butter, melted

- Lightly grease an 8-inch-square casserole dish. Combine sweet potatoes, sugar, salt, and butter until smooth.

- Lightly beat eggs and milk and stir into potato mixture. Add vanilla. Pour into baking dish. In small bowl mix brown sugar, flour, and pecans until evenly distributed. Add melted butter and toss with fork to make a crumbly mixture.

- Sprinkle crumb mixture over top of sweet potatoes. Bake at 350° for 35 minutes or until topping is browned.

PREP TIME: 10 MINUTES   COOKING TIME: 25 MINUTES

Spinach & Artichoke Bake

MAKES 6 SERVINGS

Artichokes give this spinach dish a royal treatment, and the hot sauce gives it plenty of heat. Use the hot sauce sparingly if you like a milder taste.

1/2 cup butter

3/4 cup chopped onion

2 10-ounce packages frozen chopped spinach, drained well

2 14-ounce cans artichoke hearts, drained and chopped

2 teaspoons hot sauce

1 tablespoon lemon juice

1 teaspoon Worcestershire sauce

3 cups sour cream

1/2 teaspoon garlic powder

1/2 teaspoon salt

1/4 teaspoon pepper

3/4 cup grated Parmesan cheese

3/4 cup bread crumbs

- Sauté onion in butter until onion is translucent. Add spinach and artichokes and mix well. Cook on low about 5 minutes and set aside.

- In a separate bowl, mix hot sauce, lemon juice, Worcestershire sauce, sour cream, garlic powder, salt, and pepper.

- Pour the sour cream mixture into skillet with spinach and artichokes and mix well. Pour mixture into a lightly greased 2-quart baking dish and spread Parmesan and bread crumbs over top.

- Bake at 350° for about 20 minutes or until heated throughout.

PREP TIME: 10 MINUTES   COOKING TIME: 40 MINUTES

Spinach Special

MAKES 6 SERVINGS

This spinach dish will surely make just about anyone a spinach fan.

2 16-ounce packages frozen chopped spinach
1 onion, chopped
1 stick butter
8-ounce package cream cheese, cubed
1 teaspoon seasoned salt
1/2 teaspoon black pepper
14-ounce can artichokes, drained and chopped
2/3 cup grated Parmesan cheese

• In a saucepan, cook spinach according to directions; drain thoroughly. Set aside.

• In a skillet, sauté onion in butter; cook until onion is clear, but not browned. Add cream cheese, and cook on low heat, stirring constantly until cream cheese is melted. Stir in spinach, seasonings, and artichokes.

• Pour into a lightly greased 2-quart baking dish. Sprinkle Parmesan cheese over top of casserole. Bake at 350° for 30 minutes.

Zucchini with Goat Cheese

MAKES 4 SERVINGS

Zucchini at its finest!

2 1/2 *pounds zucchini, grated*
1/2 *teaspoon salt*
1/4 *teaspoon pepper*
3 *tablespoons olive oil, divided*
2 *tablespoons chopped green onions*
3 *cloves garlic, minced*
3 *tablespoons chopped fresh basil*
1/3 *cup chopped fresh parsley*
3 *eggs, beaten*
2 *ounces goat cheese, crumbled*
3 *tablespoons bread crumbs*

● Season zucchini with salt and pepper. Heat 2 tablespoons olive oil in skillet over medium heat and sauté onions and garlic until translucent. Add zucchini and cook about 10 minutes, stirring occasionally. Add basil and parsley and stir to mix. Remove from heat and set aside.

● Beat eggs and goat cheese in large bowl. Add zucchini mixture and stir to mix. Pour mixture into a lightly greased 2-quart baking dish. Sprinkle bread crumbs over zucchini mixture.

● Drizzle remaining 1 tablespoon of oil on top. Bake at 400° for 20 to 30 minutes or until lightly browned on top.

PREP TIME: 10 MINUTES   COOKING TIME: 35 MINUTES

Creamed Spinach Casserole

MAKES 4 SERVINGS

Nothing is healthier than the wonderful green spinach used in this recipe. The cheeses create a rich, creamy dish.

2 10-ounce packages frozen chopped spinach, thawed
1 large onion, chopped
2 cloves garlic, minced
1/2 cup butter
1 cup whipping cream
1 cup milk
3/4 cup grated Parmesan cheese
1/2 cup plain bread crumbs
1 teaspoon marjoram
1 teaspoon salt
1 teaspoon pepper
1/2 cup grated Monterey Jack cheese

● Drain all liquid from spinach. In skillet, sauté onion and garlic in butter until translucent.

● In a lightly greased baking dish, mix all ingredients except Monterey Jack cheese.

● Top casserole with Monterey Jack cheese. Bake at 350° for 30 minutes.

PREP TIME: 15 MINUTES   COOKING TIME: 50 MINUTES

Zucchini Bake

MAKES 6 SERVINGS

Zucchini is a really delicious squash. This recipe produces a creamy, rich dish that's also quick and colorful.

5 zucchini, peeled and chopped
1/2 large onion, chopped
1/2 cup grated Parmesan cheese
1 tablespoon snipped parsley
1 large clove garlic, minced
1/2 teaspoon salt
1/2 teaspoon white pepper
1/2 cup butter, melted
4 eggs, beaten
1 cup biscuit mix

● Combine zucchini, onion, Parmesan, parsley, garlic, salt, and white pepper in mixing bowl and stir well.

● Add butter, beaten eggs, and biscuit mix and blend well. Pour mixture into a lightly greased 8 x 8-inch baking dish. Bake at 350° for 40 to 50 minutes.

PREP TIME: 15 MINUTES   COOKING TIME: 55 MINUTES

Zucchini, Squash & Tomato Casserole

MAKES 8 SERVINGS

Adding flavored stuffing to fancy vegetables produces the best of the best.

4 yellow squash, cubed

4 zucchini, cubed

1 onion, chopped

1 teaspoon black pepper

1 teaspoon oregano

12-ounce carton small-curd cottage cheese, drained

2 eggs

1/4 cup mayonnaise

4 Roma tomatoes, sliced

12 ounces shredded Cheddar cheese

6-ounce box chicken stuffing mix

1/4 cup grated Parmesan cheese

- In a saucepan, steam squash, zucchini, and onion until tender. Sprinkle vegetables with black pepper and oregano. Place squash mixture in a lightly greased 9 x 13-inch baking dish.

- Combine cottage cheese, eggs, and mayonnaise, mixing well. Pour cottage cheese mixture over squash mixture. Add a layer of sliced tomatoes on top of cottage cheese mixture.

- Sprinkle Cheddar cheese on top of tomatoes. Add stuffing mix on top of cheese. Top with Parmesan cheese. Bake at 325° for 45 minutes.

PREP TIME: 15 MINUTES   COOKING TIME: 45 MINUTES

Stuffed Squash

MAKES 4 TO 6 SERVINGS

This stuffing works well in just about any type of squash. The wonderful combination of seasonings promises a savory dining experience.

4 straight neck, crooked neck, patty pan, cocozelle,
  or zucchini squash
4 to 5 tablespoons butter, divided
2 tablespoons chopped onion
2 tablespoons minced celery
1 teaspoon salt
1/2 teaspoon pepper
1/2 teaspoon paprika, divided
1/4 teaspoon nutmeg
1 cup bread crumbs, divided
1 cup grated Cheddar cheese, divided
1 egg, beaten

- Make a short cut horizontally along the center line of the squashes. Gradually hollow out interior of squashes, leaving about 1/2 inch inside the shell. Reserve the pulp and set aside.

- In a skillet, melt 2 tablespoons butter and sauté onion and celery until tender and translucent. Add salt, pepper, 1/4 teaspoon paprika, nutmeg, and pulp from squash. Mix with onion and celery until heated throughout. Remove from heat and add half the bread crumbs, half the cheese, and the egg to the skillet. Stir to mix and set aside.

- Rub inside and outside of squash shells with 1 tablespoon butter or drippings from skillet. Put shells in a greased baking dish and fill each shell with pulp–bread crumb mixture. Put baking dish in a roasting pan containing several inches of water and place in oven. Bake at 350° for 15 to 20 minutes.

- Remove from oven and sprinkle remaining bread crumbs or cracker crumbs, remaining 2 tablespoons butter, remaining grated cheese, and remaining 1/4 teaspoon paprika over top. Return to oven until cheese has melted and is lightly browned.

PREP TIME: 15 MINUTES   COOKING TIME: 1 HOUR 15 MINUTES

Summer Squash Casserole

MAKES 6 SERVINGS

The summer squash family goes back 2,000 years. It doesn't need a long cooking time and can be eaten cooked or raw. This recipe is topped off with seasoned bread crumbs and pecans that give the squash a crispy touch.

1 1/4 *cups butter, divided*
1 1/2 *large onions, chopped*
3/4 *cup chopped green bell pepper*
3/4 *cup chopped red bell pepper*
1 *clove garlic, chopped*
4 *cups yellow squash or any summer squash*
2 *cups grated sharp Cheddar cheese, divided*
3 *eggs, lightly beaten*
1 2/3 *cups chopped pecans, divided*
1/8 *teaspoon hot sauce*
1 *cup seasoned bread crumbs*

● In a large skillet, melt 1/4 cup butter and sauté onions and bell peppers until soft. Add garlic and heat thoroughly.

● In a large pot, bring water to a boil with a pinch of salt. Add the squash and cook until tender, approximately 5 to 7 minutes. Drain the water and mash squash.

● Add 1/2 cup butter, 1 cup cheese, eggs, and the sautéed onion mixture to the mashed squash. Stir in 1 cup pecans and hot sauce. Stir until all ingredients are well blended.

● In a large, lightly greased baking dish, pour in squash mixture; mix the remaining cheese, pecans, and bread crumbs.

● Spread bread crumb mixture evenly over casserole. Use remaining butter to dot the top of the bread crumb mixture. Bake at 350° for 45 minutes to 1 hour, until lightly golden.

PREP TIME: 15 MINUTES   COOKING TIME: 1 HOUR 10 MINUTES

Spinach & Cheese Bake

MAKES 6 SERVINGS

This spinach is seasoned to perfection and the cheese creates a creamy texture.

3 10-ounce packages of frozen chopped spinach,
    thawed, drained thoroughly
1³/4 cups grated Cheddar cheese
16-ounce carton cottage cheese, drained
3 eggs, beaten
1/4 teaspoon salt
Pepper
1 stick butter
3 tablespoons flour
1 onion, chopped

● Preheat oven to 350°, then roll spinach in paper towels to drain thoroughly. In mixing bowl, mix together spinach, Cheddar cheese, cottage cheese, eggs, salt, and pepper.

● In a large skillet, melt butter and stir in flour until smooth. Add onions and stir.

● Spread spinach mixture in a 7 x 11-inch baking dish. Pour onion mixture over spinach mixture and stir to mix well. Bake covered for 1 hour.

PREP TIME: 10 MINUTES   MARINATING TIME: 2 HOURS   COOKING TIME: 40 MINUTES

Vegetable Roast

MAKES 6 SERVINGS

A medley of fresh vegetables combined with a flavorful marinade creates this mouthwatering casserole.

1 tablespoon balsamic vinegar

2 tablespoons olive oil

4 to 6 cloves garlic, minced

1 tablespoon thyme

1 tablespoon rosemary

1 tablespoon minced onion

1/4 teaspoon salt

1/4 teaspoon pepper

5 red potatoes, peeled, cubed

2 onions, peeled, quartered

2 red bell peppers, seeded, cut into bite-size pieces

1 yellow bell pepper, seeded, cut into bite-size pieces

1 green bell pepper, seeded, cut into bite-size pieces

2 yellow squash, cut into bite-size pieces

2 zucchini, cut into bite-size pieces

1 cup grated Parmesan cheese

- Make a marinade by stirring together vinegar, olive oil, garlic, thyme, rosemary, onion, salt, and pepper. Arrange vegetables in a lightly greased 9 x 13-inch baking dish.

- Pour marinade over vegetables and stir to coat pieces. Marinate for 2 to 3 hours and stir occasionally. Discard marinade, and bake at 400° for 30 to 40 minutes. Sprinkle with Parmesan and serve.

PREP TIME: 25 MINUTES   COOKING TIME: 40 MINUTES

Vegetable Bake

MAKES 8 SERVINGS

Here's the perfect basic vegetable casserole recipe. It's great when made as directed, but even better when you add your favorite in-season vegetables.

6 to 8 potatoes, peeled, quartered, and cooked
8-ounces sour cream
6 tablespoons butter, divided
2 tablespoons milk
1 teaspoon salt, divided
1/4 teaspoon black pepper, divided
10-ounce package frozen squash, thawed, drained
10-ounce package frozen chopped spinach, thawed,
   drained
1 egg
1 tablespoon minced onion
1/2 cup shredded Cheddar cheese

● Combine potatoes, sour cream, 2 tablespoons butter, milk, 1/2 teaspoon salt, and 1/8 teaspoon pepper. With an electric mixer, beat until smooth.

● In a separate bowl, mix squash, 2 tablespoons butter, 1/2 teaspoon salt, and 1/8 teaspoon pepper. Set aside. In another bowl, mix together spinach, egg, onion, and 2 tablespoons butter.

● In a lightly greased 2-quart baking dish, spread half the potato mixture, half the squash, and half the spinach in layers. Spread the remaining potatoes, squash, and spinach in the dish in layers.

● Bake uncovered at 350° for 30 to 40 minutes or until thoroughly heated. Spread cheese over top and return to oven for several minutes to melt the cheese.

PREP TIME: 30 MINUTES   COOKING TIME: 1 HOUR

Vegetable Casserole

MAKES 8 SERVINGS

What a fabulous combination of vegetables with a sauce to die for. Enjoy!

1 cup sliced carrots

1 cup green beans

1 cup diced potatoes

1/2 cup diced celery

2 tomatoes, cut in wedges

1 yellow squash, sliced

1 zucchini, sliced

1 small onion, chopped

1/2 head cauliflower, broken into florets

1/4 cup green bell pepper strips

1/4 cup red bell pepper strips

1/2 cup green peas

Sauce:

1 cup beef stock

1/3 cup olive oil

3 cloves garlic, minced

1/2 dried bay leaf

1/2 teaspoon tarragon

2 teaspoons salt

1 teaspoon ground pepper

● Mix vegetables in a lightly greased 9 x 13-inch pan. In a saucepan, boil sauce ingredients. Remove bay leaf. Pour over vegetables. Cover with aluminum foil and bake at 350° for 1 hour.

PREP TIME: 20 MINUTES   COOKING TIME: 30 MINUTES

Tomato & Zucchini Pie

MAKES 6 SERVINGS

This casserole comes out like a vegetable pot pie with a well-seasoned pie crust.

2 cups zucchini, chopped

2 large tomatoes, chopped and drained

1 small onion, chopped

1/3 cup grated mozzarella cheese

3/4 cup biscuit baking mix

3 eggs

1/2 teaspoon salt

1/4 teaspoon white pepper

1 1/2 cups milk

● Lightly grease a 10-inch, deep-dish pie plate with nonstick cooking spray. Mix zucchini, tomatoes, onion, and cheese together in pie plate.

● In a mixing bowl, beat baking mix, eggs, salt, white pepper, and milk until well blended. Pour over vegetables. Bake at 400° for 30 minutes.

PREP TIME: 10 MINUTES   COOKING TIME: 1 HOUR 20 MINUTES

Braised Onion with Celery

MAKES 6 SERVINGS

3 1/2 pounds onions, halved lengthwise and cut crosswise into 1/2-inch-thick slices

1/2 cup olive oil

Salt and freshly ground black pepper

7 celery ribs, cut diagonally into 1/2-inch-thick slices

● In a large skillet, cook the onions in the oil, covered, over medium heat and stirring occasionally, for 45 minutes. Season with salt and pepper and continue cooking, uncovered, over high heat, stirring occasionally, for 30 minutes, until onions are softened and golden brown. Add the celery and cook the mixture for 5 minutes, until celery begins to soften. Adjust seasoning to taste.

COOKS' TIP:

If you are out of red onions, use a sweet onion.

PREP TIME: 20 MINUTES   COOKING TIME: 1 HOUR 10 MINUTES

Ratatouille with Feta Cheese

MAKES 6 SERVINGS

Mediterranean style: This old-world favorite is full to the brim with eggplant and fresh basil flavors. Few dishes adapt better to unattended slow cooking.

3 tablespoons olive oil

4 cloves garlic, minced

1 1/2 pound eggplant, peeled and cut into
   1/2-inch cubes

1 yellow pepper, thinly sliced

2 medium onions, halved and sliced

1 medium zucchini, thinly sliced

1 tablespoon chopped fresh lemon thyme leaves

3 tablespoons chopped fresh basil

1 cup crushed tomatoes

16-ounce can stewed tomatoes, strained

1 cup low-sodium beef broth

1 teaspoon white wine vinegar

2 ounces feta cheese, crumbled

● Butter a 9 x 13-inch casserole dish. In a large saucepan, heat olive oil and sauté garlic, eggplant, and pepper until vegetables are tender. Combine onions and zucchini with the cooked vegetables, stirring in the thyme and basil.

● Spoon the mixture into the casserole dish, mixing in the tomatoes, broth, and vinegar. Bake at 350° for 1 hour. Remove casserole from oven, top with feta cheese, and bake for 5 more minutes until cheese begins to melt.

PREP TIME: 25 MINUTES   COOKING TIME: 45 MINUTES

Chili-Stuffed Chayote Squash

MAKES 6 SERVINGS

Chipotle chili revs up the flavor—and the heat—of the mild, chayote squash in this colorful recipe. Tame the flame with sour cream.

3 *chayote squashes or small zucchini, halved*

1 *tamarillo, peeled and sliced*

1 *small onion, quartered*

4 *cloves garlic, halved*

2 *tablespoons minced fresh sage*

1 *chipotle chili, seeded and chopped*

2 *tablespoons recaito sauce*

Vegetable oil

6 *sprigs fresh cilantro, chopped*

6 *tablespoons sour cream*

● Preheat oven to 350°. Scoop the pulp from the squashes, reserving the pulp and leaving 1/2-inch thick shells. Combine the pulp, tamarillo, onions, garlic, sage, and chipotle in a food processor. Process until finely chopped. Stir in the recaito sauce. Spoon into the squash shells.

● Arrange the shells in an oiled casserole dish. Bake covered for 30 minutes. Remove cover and continue baking 15 minutes longer. Serve topped with the cilantro and sour cream.

COOKS' TIP:

Chipotle chilies are smoked, dried jalapeño peppers. If you can't find them, substitute another dried hot pepper. Look for recaito sauce, which is similar to sofrito, in the international section of large supermarkets.

PREP TIME: 20 MINUTES   COOKING TIME: 35 MINUTES

Winter Vegetable Stew with Cheddar and Croutons

MAKES 4 TO 6 SERVINGS

A hearty, flavorful stew for healthy appetites. And it's vitamin A–okay, courtesy of the carrots and broccoli.

1/4 cup olive oil

2 cloves garlic, chopped

2 carrots, diagonally sliced 1/2-inch thick

1 celery stalk, diagonally sliced 11/2-inch thick

1 leek, white part only, sliced 1/2 inch thick

1 potato, cut into 1/2-inch cubes

1 turnip, cut into 1/2-inch cubes

14-ounce can low-sodium chicken broth

1 teaspoon dried savory

Salt and freshly ground black pepper to taste

1/4 pound broccoli florets

3 cups toasted croutons

1 cup shredded Cheddar cheese

Bacon-flavored bits, for garnish

● In a large saucepan or Dutch oven, heat the oil and sauté garlic until slightly golden. Add the carrots, celery, and leek, sautéing until tender, about 5 minutes. Add the potato, turnip, broth, savory, and salt and pepper to taste, stirring to combine vegetables. Bring to a boil and simmer, covered, for 20 minutes.

● Add the broccoli. Cover and cook until the broccoli is tender, about 10 more minutes. Divide the stew among 4 bowls; top each serving with croutons, cheese, and bacon-flavored bits.

PREP TIME: 15 MINUTES   COOKING TIME: 1 HOUR 15 MINUTES

Black Bean & Corn Chili

MAKES 4 TO 6 SERVINGS

Create a stir with knockout chili that's full of beans and healthful vegetables.

3 tablespoons vegetable oil

4 cloves garlic, minced

2 large onions, chopped

1 large green bell pepper, chopped

15 1/2-ounce can black beans, rinsed and drained

28-ounce can tomatoes, cut up with liquid

1 1/2-cups low-sodium chicken or vegetable broth

1 chili pepper, seeded and chopped

2 tablespoons chili powder

2 teaspoons ground cumin

1 teaspoon dried oregano

1 1/2 cups corn

• In a large saucepan or Dutch oven, heat the oil and sauté garlic and onions until slightly golden, about 8 minutes. Add the green pepper and sauté for 2 minutes longer. Stir in the beans, tomatoes, broth, chili pepper, chili powder, cumin, and oregano, and bring to a boil. Reduce heat, cover, and simmer for about 1 hour.

• Add the corn to the chili and cook until corn is heated through, about 5 minutes longer. Adjust the seasonings and serve over white rice.

PREP TIME: 20 MINUTES   COOKING TIME: 30 MINUTES

Braised Winter Root Vegetables

MAKES 6 SERVINGS

3 large carrots, trimmed and peeled

4 large parsnips, trimmed and peeled

2 large leeks, white parts only, cleaned

2 small fennel bulbs, trimmed

1/4 cup butter

2 large garlic cloves, crushed

1/2 teaspoon dried thyme

pinch sugar

salt and freshly ground black pepper to taste

1/3 cup dry white wine

• Cut the carrots and parsnips into 2 x 1/2-inch lengths. Cut leeks crosswise into 1/2-inch rounds. Cut fennel bulbs lengthwise into 8 wedges.

• In a large saucepan over medium heat, melt 3 tablespoons of the butter. Sauté the carrots, parsnips, leeks, fennel, garlic, thyme, sugar, and salt and pepper to taste, for 5 to 10 minutes. Add the wine and simmer, covered, stirring occasionally for 15 to 20 minutes, or until the vegetables are tender. Stir in the remaining tablespoon of butter and adjust seasoning.

Eggs, Cheese & More

PREP TIME: 15 MINUTES   COOKING TIME: 30–45 MINUTES

Spinach Quiche

MAKES 6 SERVINGS

This is a great dish to serve at a luncheon. You will want to make this quiche often, so invest in a metal quiche pan that has a removable bottom.

10-ounce package frozen chopped spinach

9-inch pastry shell

1/4 cup grated Parmesan cheese

3 eggs, beaten

1 1/2 cups cottage cheese, drained

1 cup heavy cream

2 tablespoons minced onion

1 1/2 teaspoons salt

1/2 teaspoon pepper

1 teaspoon caraway seeds

1/4 teaspoon nutmeg

1/2 teaspoon Worcestershire sauce

3 drops Tabasco

3 tablespoons butter, melted

● Cook spinach according to package directions and drain thoroughly. Bake the pastry shell at 400° for 8 minutes. Cool. Reduce oven temperature to 350°.

● Sprinkle parmesan cheese in bottom of shell. Combine spinach and all remaining ingredients except butter in shell. Melt butter and pour over top.

● Bake for 30 to 45 minutes or until toothpick comes out clean.

PREP TIME: 10 MINUTES   COOKING TIME: 45 MINUTES

Quick Brunch Bake

MAKES 6 SERVINGS

A touch of nutmeg enhances the aroma and flavor of spinach; so for that special touch, sprinkle a little nutmeg over this casserole just before serving.

1 cup seasoned bread crumbs, divided
2 10-ounce packages frozen chopped spinach, thawed
24-ounce carton small curd cottage cheese
3/4 cup grated Parmesan cheese
5 eggs

- Grease an 8 x 8-inch baking dish and spread one-fourth of the bread crumbs over bottom. Bake at 350° for 5 minutes or until slightly brown.

- Drain spinach by rolling it in paper towels and squeezing until thoroughly drained. Mix spinach with cottage cheese, Parmesan, and 3 beaten eggs and spread over bread crumbs.

- Beat remaining eggs and pour over mixture. Bake covered at 350° for 40 to 45 minutes or until a fork inserted in center comes out clean. Let cool slightly to make slicing easier.

PREP TIME: 15 MINUTES (REFRIGERATE OVERNIGHT)
COOKING TIME: 45 MINUTES

Good Morning Sausage

MAKES 6 SERVINGS

This casserole calls for hot biscuits and strawberry preserves.

1 pound pork sausage
6 eggs, beaten
2 cups milk
6 slices bread, cubed
1 teaspoon dry mustard
1 teaspoon salt
1 cup grated Cheddar cheese
1/8 teaspoon oregano

- In skillet, brown sausage and drain. Mix all ingredients together. Place in a greased 9 x 13-inch casserole dish.

- Cover and refrigerate for several hours or overnight. Bake at 350° for 45 minutes or until mixture is brown around edges.

Egg McMaster

MAKES 10–12 SERVINGS

The red bell pepper adds a good flavor to these eggs and also makes an attractive, colorful dish! Leftovers can be warmed the next day.

24 eggs
1/2 cup milk
1/3 cup butter
1/2 cup sherry
3 4-ounce cans mushrooms, drained
1 red bell pepper, chopped
2 10-ounce cans cream of mushroom soup
1/4 teaspoon salt
2 cups grated Cheddar cheese

● Beat eggs and milk to scramble. Melt butter in skillet. Add eggs and lightly scramble. Pour into a greased 9 x 13-inch baking dish.

● In a separate bowl, mix together sherry, mushrooms, bell pepper, soup, and salt. Pour over eggs and sprinkle cheese over mixture. Refrigerate covered for 10 to 12 hours. Bake at 350° for 20 to 25 minutes.

PREP TIME: 25 MINUTES (REFRIGERATE OVERNIGHT)   COOKING TIME: 1 HOUR

Apple & Sausage Breakfast Casserole

MAKES 6 SERVINGS

Because this casserole needs to sit overnight before baking, you can sleep in and have a fabulous breakfast, too. Before baking in the morning, let casserole stand at room temperature for 20 to 25 minutes. Delicious served with hot biscuits!

2 *pounds ground pork sausage*
8 *slices bread*
1 1/2 *cups sliced apples*
2/3 *teaspoons dry mustard*
8 *eggs, lightly beaten*
1 1/2 *cups grated sharp Cheddar cheese*
3 *cups milk*

• In a large skillet, fry the sausage, breaking it into small bits as it cooks. Drain on paper towels, reserving some of the fat. Lightly grease a 9 x 13-inch baking dish. Place the sausage in the baking dish.

• Remove the crust from the bread and tear it into small pieces or cut into cubes. Sauté the apples in the sausage fat. In a large bowl, combine the apples, bread, mustard, eggs, cheese, and milk until well mixed.

• Pour apple mixture over the sausage. Cover with foil and refrigerate overnight. In the morning, bake covered at 350° for 30 minutes. Remove the foil and bake uncovered for an additional 30 minutes.

PREP TIME: 10 MINUTES   COOKING TIME: 20 MINUTES

Southern Cheese Grits

MAKES 4 SERVINGS

You haven't had breakfast in New Orleans if you haven't had grits served with your eggs!

1 1/2 cups milk

3 1/2 cups water

1/2 teaspoon salt

1 1/4 cups quick grits

1/2 cup butter

6-ounce roll garlic cheese

3 cups shredded Cheddar or Colby cheese

1/2 teaspoon cayenne

1/2 teaspoon garlic salt

1 tablespoon Worcestershire sauce

Paprika

● Boil milk, water, and salt in a medium saucepan. Add grits and stir to mix. Reduce heat and cook until desired doneness. (Make sure heat is low enough so grits won't stick to bottom of pan.) Stir several times.

● Add butter and cheeses and stir to melt. Add cayenne, garlic salt, and Worcestershire sauce. Stir well.

● Pour into a lightly greased 3-quart casserole and sprinkle with paprika. Bake covered at 350° for 15 to 20 minutes or until thoroughly heated.

PREP TIME: 20 MINUTES   COOKING TIME: 1 HOUR 45 MINUTES

Baked Potato Sunrise

MAKES 4 SERVINGS

Perk up any meal with these "twice baked" potatoes! (To speed up the cooking process, push metal skewers through center to conduct heat.)

4 Idaho baking potatoes
Olive oil or butter
1/2 pound hot, ground pork sausage
1 cup chopped green onion with tops, divided
1/4 cup minced red bell pepper
1/4 cup heavy cream
3 egg yolks
1/4 cup sour cream
1 teaspoon salt
1/2 teaspoon white pepper
Hungarian paprika
Fresh parsley
Fresh tomato slices

- Wash potatoes and stick skin several times with fork. Rub skin with a little oil or butter and arrange on baking sheet. Bake at 350° for 1 hour 30 minutes or until potatoes are soft on the inside. Remove potatoes from oven to cool.

- Brown sausage in skillet until crumbly and cooked through. Drain sausage on paper towels and transfer to large mixing bowl. Add a little oil to skillet and sauté 3/4 cup green onion and red bell pepper until tender and translucent. Add onion and bell pepper to sausage in mixing bowl.

- When potatoes are cool enough to touch, cut small oval in outer skin on top of potato. With a small spoon, scoop out pulp, being careful to leave shell intact. Leave about 1/4-inch thickness inside outer skin.

- Put potato pulp in a separate bowl and mash with a fork or potato masher. Slowly stir in heavy cream, egg yolks, sour cream, salt, and white pepper. Stir well to mix ingredients and to make a creamy texture. Add a little more cream if mixture seems too dry.

- Slowly fold in sausage-onion mixture and stir to combine. Spoon this filling into individual potato shells, allowing filling to rise above top of potato skin. Place stuffed potatoes back on baking sheet and sprinkle top of each potato with paprika.

- Bake at 350° for 10 to 15 minutes to heat thoroughly. Remove from oven and garnish with parsley and remaining minced green onion tops. Serve with tomato slices on the side.

PREP TIME: 10 MINUTES   COOKING TIME: 50 MINUTES

Bacon-Spinach Quiche

MAKES 8 SERVINGS

This quiche is not only great for a brunch, it is great for lunch.

2 9-inch deep-dish, unbaked pie shells

3 tablespoons butter, softened

2 10-ounce packages frozen chopped spinach, thawed

1 pound bacon, cooked

2 cups heavy cream

8 eggs, beaten

2/3 cup shredded Swiss cheese

3/4 teaspoon salt

1/8 teaspoon ground nutmeg

● Prepare pie shells by rubbing butter on inside bottom and sides of deep dish pie plates. Drain spinach by putting between several layers of paper towels and squeezing liquid out.

● Layer spinach in both pie shells and crumble cooked bacon on top. Whisk together cream, eggs, cheese, and seasonings, and pour over spinach and bacon. Bake at 425° for 10 minutes. Reduce heat to 325° and bake 35 to 40 minutes longer. Quiche is done when a knife inserted in the center comes out clean.

PREP TIME: 15 MINUTES   COOKING TIME: 35 MINUTES

Sausage and Chile Bake

MAKES 6 SERVINGS

This breakfast casserole can be made the night before and refrigerated. Allow an extra 5 minutes of baking time.

7-ounce can whole green chilies
1 pound hot sausage, cooked, crumbled
2 tablespoons dried onion flakes
5 eggs, lightly beaten
1 pint half-and-half
2/3 cup shredded Parmesan cheese
1/2 cup grated Swiss cheese
1/2 teaspoon seasoned salt

• Butter a 9 x 13-inch baking dish and line the bottom with split and seeded green chilies. Sprinkle sausage over chilies.

• In a medium bowl, combine onion flakes, eggs, half-and-half, cheeses, and seasoned salt. Pour over the sausage and bake uncovered at 350° for 35 minutes or until top is lightly browned.

• Allow to set for 5 to 10 minutes before slicing and serving.

PREP TIME: 10 MINUTES   COOKING TIME: 45 MINUTES

Mexican Quiche

MAKES 6 SERVINGS

1 1/2 pounds ground beef
1 envelope taco seasoning mix
10-inch deep-dish pie shell, baked
2 cups grated Monterey Jack cheese
2 cups grated Cheddar cheese
4 eggs, lightly beaten with 1 cup milk
Salsa

• Brown ground beef until crumbly, then drain. Mix in taco seasoning and stir. In baked pie shell, sprinkle half the cheeses over bottom.

• Spoon in beef mixture evenly and sprinkle remaining cheeses on top. Pour mixture of eggs and milk on top.

• Bake at 350° for 30 to 45 minutes or until golden brown. Serve with salsa on the side.

PREP TIME: 5 MINUTES   COOKING TIME: 30 MINUTES

Cheesy Zucchini
Frittata

MAKES 6 SERVINGS

Although frittatas are famous for their savory herbs and spices, the zucchini and carrots in this recipe add a flavor of their own.

4 eggs

4 cups shredded zucchini

2 cups peeled, shredded carrots

1/2 cup flour

3/4 cup mayonnaise

1 cup shredded Monterey Jack cheese

1/2 cup grated Parmesan cheese

1/4 cup chopped onion

1 teaspoon basil

Pepper to taste

- Beat eggs in mixing bowl. Fold in zucchini, carrots, flour, mayonnaise, cheeses, onion, basil, and pepper.

- Pour into a buttered quiche pan and bake at 375° for 30 minutes or until set.

PREP TIME: 15 MINUTES   COOKING TIME: 30 MINUTES

Mexican Brunch

MAKES 6 SERVINGS

This is a meal in itself—you don't need biscuits or toast. Serve with fruit to add a light touch to this spicy casserole.

10$1/2$-ounce can mushroom soup

4-ounce can chopped green chilies, drained

7-ounce can green chili salsa

1 cup sour cream

$1/2$ teaspoon coriander

$1/2$ teaspoon ground cumin

1-pound package hot ground pork sausage

4 tablespoons butter

7 eggs, beaten

$1/2$ cup small-curd cottage cheese, drained

$1/2$ cup chopped green onion tops

8 12-inch flour tortillas, buttered

1$1/2$ cups grated Cheddar cheese

1 cup grated Monterey Jack cheese

• In a mixing bowl, whisk together mushroom soup, green chilies, salsa, sour cream, coriander, and cumin; set aside. Brown sausage and crumble it while it cooks. Drain thoroughly; set aside.

• In skillet over low heat, melt butter, then add the eggs. Stir in cottage cheese and green onions. Add 3 tablespoons of mushroom-green chili sauce and all the crumbled sausage. Mix thoroughly until set and remove from heat.

• Spread a small amount of sauce over bottom of a lightly greased 9 x 13-inch baking dish. Spoon egg-sausage mixture into eight flour tortillas and roll them up. Place in baking dish with seam side down. Cover with remaining sauce.

• Sprinkle Cheddar cheese and Monterey Jack cheese over top of sauce. Bake at 350° for 25 to 30 minutes or until cheeses are bubbly.

PREP TIME: 15 MINUTES   COOKING TIME: 1 HOUR 5 MINUTES

Breakfast Potatoes

MAKES 6 SERVINGS

This is a hearty start for the day—and a lot healthier than "hash browns." Serve with some fresh fruit and a buttered hot biscuit.

9-inch unbaked pie shell

1 pound mild or hot sausage

16-ounce carton small curd cottage cheese

3 eggs

2 1/2 cups well seasoned warm, mashed potatoes

2/3 cup sour cream

1/4 stick margarine, melted

1 teaspoon dried oregano

1/4 teaspoon garlic powder

1/2 teaspoon seasoned salt

1/8 teaspoon cayenne pepper

2 1/4 cups shredded Cheddar cheese

Salsa

- In a 375° oven, bake pie shell for 7 minutes. Set aside.

- Crumble the sausage into skillet and cook thoroughly; drain well.

- Place the cottage cheese and eggs in a food processor. Process until well blended. Pour into a large bowl; add the potatoes, sour cream, margarine, and seasonings, mixing well.

- Spoon the sausage into the pie shell. Pour potato mixture over sausage. Sprinkle with cheese.

- Bake uncovered at 350° for about 55 minutes. To serve, cut in pie wedge shapes and serve with salsa.

PREP TIME: 15 MINUTES   COOKING TIME: 55 MINUTES

Yellow Squash & Sausage Mix

MAKES 8 SERVINGS

Summer gardens produce the most beautiful squash. When buying yellow squash, choose the smallest ones since they have fewer seeds.

2 pounds yellow squash, cut into bite-size pieces
1/4 cup chopped onion
1 pound Italian sausage
1/2 cup fine cracker crumbs
2 eggs, beaten
1/2 cup grated Parmesan cheese, divided
1/4 teaspoon thyme
1/4 teaspoon rosemary
1/4 teaspoon garlic powder
Salt and pepper to taste

• Cook squash in boiling, salted water until tender; drain. In skillet, brown onion and sausage; drain.

• Add squash and remaining ingredients to onion and sausage, except 2 tablespoons Parmesan cheese, mixing well.

• Divide mixture between 2 greased 8-inch pie plates. Sprinkle with remaining Parmesan cheese. Bake at 350° for 45 minutes, or until brown.

Chicken & Turkey Casseroles & Stews

Chardonnay Chicken •
Chicken-Mushroom Stroganoff •
Chicken & Spinach Casserole •
Chicken Lasagna •
Chicken Fiesta •
Chicken and Rice Casserole •
Tortilla Bake •
Chicken and Crab Divan •
Chicken, Cheese, and •
Vegetable Casserole
Chicken-Avocado Casserole •
Oven-Baked Chicken •
Chicken-Cheese Casserole •
Creamy Chicken & Macaroni •
Chicken Tetrazzini •
Chicken Bake •
Zesty Chicken Bake •
Artichoke Chicken Casserole •
Chicken Enchiladas •

• Poppy Seed Chicken
• Chicken Camarillo
• Creamy Chicken & Ham
• Chicken Linguine
• Coq au Vin
• Orange Baked Quail
• Chicken Creole
• Provençal Chicken Stew
• Home-Style Chicken Stew with
Mushrooms and Peppers
• Hungarian Cabbage & Chicken
• Rustic Chicken Stew
• Turkey Cornbread
• Turkey, Carrot, and Apple Stew
• Rustic Chicken
• Louisiana Chicken Gumbo
• Chicken Posole
• South American Chicken, Corn &
Potato Stew

Chardonnay Chicken

MAKES 6 TO 8 SERVINGS

Invite the new neighbors over for this scrumptious chicken dinner and you'll have friends for life.

3 onions, sliced thinly

1 bell pepper, chopped

2 cloves garlic, minced

1/4 cup butter, melted, plus extra butter for sautéing

7 to 8 boneless, skinless chicken breast halves

Salt

Pepper

Garlic powder

14-ounce can artichoke bottoms, halved, drained

2 1/4 cups grated Gruyère cheese

2 cups bread crumbs

1 tablespoon tarragon

1 bottle Chardonnay wine

● Sauté onions, bell pepper, and garlic in butter until tender and translucent. Spoon two-thirds of mixture into a lightly greased 9 x 13-inch baking dish and spread over bottom of dish.

● Sprinkle both sides of chicken pieces with salt, pepper, and a little garlic powder and place over onion–bell pepper mixture. Scatter artichoke hearts over chicken, then remaining onion mixture.

● In a separate bowl, mix together cheese, bread crumbs, tarragon, and melted butter and pour over chicken. Pour wine into dish to cover chicken halfway. Cover baking dish and refrigerate over night.

● To prepare, bake at 350° for 20 minutes; remove cover and bake another 20 minutes until bubbly and golden brown on top. Don't overcook.

PREP TIME: 20 MINUTES   COOKING TIME: 40 MINUTES

Chicken-Mushroom Stroganoff

MAKES 4 SERVINGS

A new twist for stroganoff.

8 boneless, skinless chicken breast halves

Salt

Pepper

1/2 cup butter, divided

2 onions, quartered

1/2 pound mushrooms, stemmed, chopped

1 tablespoon flour

1/2 cup chicken broth

1/2 cup dry white wine

1/2 cup sour cream

3 tablespoons Dijon mustard

Cooked rice

Parsley

• Season both sides of chicken with salt and pepper and cut into bite-size pieces. Sauté in skillet with half the butter until lightly brown on the outside.

• Simmer about 5 to 10 minutes more until opaque, stirring occasionally. Remove chicken from heat and set aside in baking dish with lid to keep warm.

• Sauté onions and mushrooms until tender and translucent. Pour into chicken mixture and cover with lid. Melt remaining butter in skillet and add flour, stirring continuously for about 3 minutes to remove lumps. Whisk in broth and wine, stirring constantly to thicken sauce.

• Cook for about 5 minutes, then add sour cream and mustard. Simmer for another 5 minutes and stir occasionally to mix and heat throughout. Pour over chicken and warm in oven about 5 to 10 minutes. Serve over rice and garnish with parsley.

Chicken & Spinach Casserole

MAKES 6 TO 8 SERVINGS

Delicious—that's what it is!

6 to 8 boneless, skinless chicken breast halves

10-ounce package of egg noodles

1/4 cup butter

1/4 cup flour

1 cup milk

2 cups sour cream

2 teaspoons lemon juice

2 teaspoons seasoned salt

1/2 teaspoon cayenne pepper

1 teaspoon paprika

2 teaspoons pepper

1 package frozen chopped spinach, cooked, drained

6-ounce can sliced mushrooms, undrained

4-ounce can sliced water chestnuts, drained

4-ounce jar pimientos, drained, chopped

1/2 cup chopped onion

1/2 cup chopped celery

1 1/2 cups grated Monterey Jack cheese

● Cook chicken in water seasoned with salt, about 10 minutes. Reserve stock and shred chicken. Cook noodles according to package directions, drain, and set aside.

● Melt butter in a large saucepan and stir in flour. Slowly add milk and 1 cup reserved chicken stock. Cook over low heat, stirring constantly, until thickened. Add sour cream, lemon juice, and seasonings, mixing well.

● Add noodles, spinach, mushrooms, water chestnuts, pimientos, onion, and celery. Spoon a layer of spinach mixture into a greased 3-quart baking dish. Add a layer of chicken. Repeat layers and top with cheese. Bake at 300° for 30 minutes or until bubbly.

PREP TIME: 25 MINUTES   COOKING TIME: 1 HOUR 10 MINUTES

Chicken Lasagna

MAKES 6 SERVINGS

This is not your average lasagna! The chicken reigns supreme!

1 pound boneless, skinless chicken breasts

1/2 cup butter

1/2 cup flour

3 cups milk

1 1/4 cups grated Parmesan cheese, divided

1 1/4 cups dry white wine

1 1/2 teaspoons salt, divided

1 teaspoon pepper, divided

1/2 teaspoon garlic powder

1/2 teaspoon Italian seasoning

1 large onion, chopped

3 tablespoons minced fresh basil

10-ounce package frozen chopped spinach, cooked

16-ounce carton ricotta cheese

2 eggs

16-ounce package lasagna noodles, cooked, drained

2 cups grated mozzarella cheese

• Cook chicken in boiling water about 10 minutes until tender. Drain, cool, and set aside. Melt butter in skillet and add in flour, stirring constantly to thicken into a paste.

• Slowly stir in milk and continue to cook until thickened. Add 1/2 cup Parmesan and stir until melted. Pour in wine and season with 1/2 teaspoon salt and 1/4 teaspoon pepper. Set aside.

• Season chicken with remaining salt, pepper, garlic powder, and Italian seasoning. Cut into bite-size pieces and place in a mixing bowl. Add onion and basil and stir to mix well. Set aside.

• Roll spinach in several paper towels to drain water thoroughly from spinach. In a separate mixing bowl, add spinach, ricotta cheese, eggs, and remaining Parmesan cheese. Stir until blended and set aside.

• In a lightly greased 9 x 13-inch baking dish, pour in 3/4 cup of white sauce. Arrange one-third of the noodles over sauce and top with spinach-ricotta mixture.

• Add another layer of noodles and another 3/4 cup sauce over noodles. Spoon chicken mixture on top, then pour 3/4 cup sauce over chicken.

• Cover with noodles and pour remaining sauce over casserole. Sprinkle mozzarella over top. Bake at 350° for 45 to 50 minutes or until bubbly and browned on top. Let stand for 10 minutes before serving.

Chicken Fiesta

MAKES 4 SERVINGS

Make this night into a celebration with a chicken fiesta dinner!

4 boneless, skinless chicken breasts
14-ounce can hearts of palm, drained
1 cup melted butter, plus more for brushing chicken
1 teaspoon salt, divided
1/2 teaspoon white pepper, divided
3 egg whites
1 tablespoon lemon juice
Fresh parsley
Hungarian paprika

● Flatten chicken breasts slightly. Wrap each one around a stalk of palm heart. Brush with melted butter and season with 1/2 teaspoon salt and 1/4 teaspoon pepper.

● Bake in a lightly greased baking dish, uncovered, at 400° for 20 to 25 minutes, basting several times with drippings. Place egg whites, lemon juice, 1/2 teaspoon salt, and 1/4 teaspoon pepper in a blender.

● With blender on, slowly drip hot melted butter into blender to make a good emulsion. Garnish chicken with parsley and paprika and pour sauce over chicken. Serve.

PREP TIME: 30 MINUTES   COOKING TIME: 45 MINUTES

Chicken and Rice Casserole

MAKES 6 SERVINGS

Except for the chicken, these ingredients all come right from your pantry (chicken from deep freezer) to make a quick meal for a sick friend, new neighbor, or when unexpected company happens along.

1 cup uncooked rice

2 1/2 cups cooked, cubed chicken

1/2 cup chopped onion

1/2 cup chopped celery

3/4 cup mayonnaise

8-ounce can sliced water chestnuts, drained

1/2 cup slivered almonds

10 1/2-ounce can cream of chicken soup

10 1/2-ounce can cream of celery soup

1/4 stick butter, melted

2 cups corn flakes, crumbled

• Cook rice according to package directions. Mix all ingredients together except butter and corn flakes and place in a lightly greased 9 x 13-inch baking dish.

• Melt butter and mix with corn flakes. Sprinkle on top of casserole. Bake at 350° for 45 minutes.

Tortilla Bake

MAKES 6 SERVINGS

Fiesta time!

2 tablespoons oil

1 tablespoon minced garlic

1/2 cup minced green onions

5 to 6 boneless, skinless chicken breast halves,
    chopped

2 15-ounce cans chicken broth

3 tablespoons cornstarch

1 1/2 cups grated Monterey Jack cheese, divided

1/2 cup sour cream

1/2 cup mayonnaise

4-ounce can chopped green chilies, drained

1/2 cup minced cilantro

1/4 cup sliced black olives

10 to 12 flour tortillas, 6 to 8 inches

• Heat oil and stir in garlic and onions. Add chicken and sauté until golden brown. In a saucepan, mix together broth and cornstarch. Boil for 1 minute, stirring constantly. Remove from heat.

• Stir in 1 cup cheese, sour cream, mayonnaise, green chilies, cilantro, and black olives. Add 3/4 cup of sauce mixture to chicken and stir to mix.

• Spoon chicken mixture into center of each tortilla and roll. Arrange rolled tortillas, seam side down, in a lightly greased 9 x 13-inch baking dish.

• Pour remaining sauce over top of tortilla rolls and sprinkle with remaining Monterey Jack cheese. Bake at 350° for 20 to 30 minutes or until heated throughout.

PREP TIME: 15 MINUTES   COOKING TIME: 45 MINUTES

Chicken and Crab Divan

MAKES 4 SERVINGS

Chicken and crab together can't be beat! And of course, the heavy cream creates a creamy, dreamy dish.

4 boneless, skinless chicken breasts

8 tablespoons butter, divided

8 ounces fresh crabmeat

1/4 cup cooking sherry

Salt and pepper to taste

1/2 cup mushrooms, sliced

1/4 cup chopped onion

3 tablespoons flour

1 1/3 cups heavy cream

1 cup milk

1/2 bunch chopped parsley

Dash cayenne pepper

1/4 cup grated Parmesan cheese

2 15-ounce cans artichoke hearts, drained

Paprika

• In skillet, cook chicken in 4 tablespoons butter for 10 minutes or until tender. Add crabmeat and cook another 5 minutes. Add sherry and allow to evaporate quickly. Season with salt and pepper. Remove chicken and crab and keep warm.

• Add remaining 4 tablespoons butter to pan drippings. Sauté mushrooms and onions. Stir in flour. Gradually add cream and milk, stirring constantly until thickened. Stir in parsley and cayenne. Remove from heat and blend in Parmesan.

• Arrange artichoke hearts on bottom of a lightly greased 8 x 12-inch baking dish. Cover with half of sauce. Add chicken-crab mixture and top with remaining sauce. Sprinkle with paprika. Bake uncovered at 375° for 20 minutes.

Chicken, Cheese, and Vegetable Casserole

MAKES 8 SERVINGS

This recipe calls for company—and the company will want to take home the leftovers.

8 boneless, skinless chicken breasts

3 8 1/2-ounce cans artichoke hearts, drained

2 8-ounce cans sliced mushrooms, drained

1 cup butter

1/2 cup flour

3 cups milk

4 ounces grated Swiss cheese

4 ounces grated Cheddar cheese

1/3 cup tomato sauce

1/2 teaspoon cayenne pepper

8 garlic cloves, minced

Salt and pepper to taste

● Boil chicken in water until cooked; drain and shred. Spray a 9 x 13-inch baking dish with cooking spray and layer artichoke hearts in bottom of dish. Layer chicken and mushrooms.

● In a saucepan, melt butter over low heat. Add the flour, blending well. Gradually add the milk and cook, stirring until smooth and creamy. Add remaining ingredients and blend.

● Pour cream sauce over the casserole and bake uncovered at 350° for 35 minutes or until bubbly.

Chicken-Avocado Casserole

MAKES 6 SERVINGS

The outstanding avocado perks up many a dish, and with chicken, this dish is tops.

1/4 cup plus 11/2 tablespoons flour

Salt and pepper to taste

1/4 teaspoon thyme

6 boneless, skinless chicken breast halves

8 tablespoons butter, divided

1 small onion, chopped

1 cup dry white wine

2/3 cup chicken broth

1 chicken bouillon cube

2/3 cup cream

3 avocados

Lemon juice

Oil

● In a bowl, mix together 1/4 cup flour, salt, pepper, and thyme. Roll chicken in mixture. In a skillet, melt 5 tablespoons butter and brown chicken. Place in a lightly greased baking dish.

● Add remaining butter to skillet and brown onion. Add wine, chicken broth, and bouillon blended with 1/2 tablespoons flour. Bring to a boil and cook until thick. Pour mixture over chicken.

● Cover and cook at 375° for 1 hour. Remove from oven. Cool slightly and stir in cream. Sprinkle peeled, sliced avocados with lemon juice. Place on chicken and brush with small amount of oil. Return to oven for 10 minutes.

PREP TIME: 15 MINUTES (REFRIGERATE OVERNIGHT)   COOKING TIME: 1 HOUR

Oven-Baked Chicken

MAKES 8 SERVINGS

This is oven-baked chicken at its best!

2 cups sour cream

1/4 cup lemon juice

5 teaspoons Worcestershire sauce

1 teaspoon celery salt

2 teaspoons paprika

4 cloves garlic, crushed

1/2 teaspoon pepper

8 boneless, skinless chicken breast halves

8-ounce package seasoned bread crumbs

2 sticks butter, melted

● Combine sour cream, lemon juice, Worcestershire, celery salt, paprika, garlic, and pepper in large bowl and mix thoroughly. Coat chicken with mixture. Cover bowl and refrigerate chicken in bowl overnight.

● Remove each piece of chicken and roll in bread crumbs. Place chicken in a lightly greased baking dish. Pour 1 stick melted butter over chicken.

● Bake covered at 350° for 45 minutes. Remove cover and pour remaining butter over chicken and cook 15 minutes longer.

Chicken-Cheese Casserole

MAKES 6 SERVINGS

When in a hurry for a quick supper, this is the recipe!

Small bag ranch-style chips
12-ounce can white chunk chicken, drained
10 1/2-ounce can cream of chicken soup
10 1/2-ounce can cream of celery soup
4-ounce can chopped green chilies
8-ounce carton sour cream
3/4 cup shredded Cheddar cheese

• Crush chips and place in a lightly greased 9 x 13-inch baking dish. In a large mixing bowl, combine chicken, soups, chilies, and sour cream, and pour over crushed chips.

• Cover and bake at 350° for 25 minutes. Uncover and sprinkle cheese over top. Return to oven for about 5 minutes or until cheese has melted.

Creamy Chicken & Macaroni

MAKES 4 SERVINGS

A meal in itself—now the kids will want chicken with their macaroni!

1 1/2 cups uncooked macaroni
1/2 stick butter, melted
1 tablespoon flour
3-ounce package cream cheese
4-ounce jar pimiento
1 teaspoon salt
1/2 teaspoon pepper
1 cup milk
14-ounce can chicken broth
3 cups cooked, cubed chicken

• Cook macaroni according to package directions; drain and set aside. In a saucepan, over low heat, combine butter, flour, cream cheese, pimiento, salt, and pepper.

• Add milk and broth, stirring constantly. Heat to boiling and cook for 3 minutes, still stirring. Add chicken and macaroni and pour into a greased, 2-quart baking dish. Bake covered at 350° for 30 minutes.

PREP TIME: 15 MINUTES COOKING TIME: 3 HOURS

Chicken Tetrazzini

MAKES 6 SERVINGS

A different tetrazzini—thick, creamy, and full of flavor!

5 quarts water

3 pounds boneless, skinless chicken breast halves

3 bacon slices, halved

2 ribs celery, chopped

2 tablespoons Creole seasoning

1 tablespoon salt

1/2 teaspoon garlic powder

1/4 teaspoon pepper

1-pound package thin spaghetti

2 10 1/2-ounce cans chicken broth (optional)

1 pound fresh mushrooms, stemmed

2 to 4 cloves garlic, minced

2 to 4 tablespoons butter

3/4 cup butter, melted

3/4 cup flour

1/2 pint heavy cream

1 1/2 cups grated Parmesan cheese, divided

• Pour water into large pot and add chicken, bacon, celery, Creole seasoning, salt, garlic powder, and pepper. Bring to a boil, cover, and simmer for about 1 1/2 hours.

• Reserve broth and cut chicken into bite-size pieces. Bring broth to a boil and add spaghetti. Cook until slightly tender. Drain spaghetti into a separate bowl to reserve broth and set aside.

• Measure remaining broth and pour into stock pot. There should be 8 to 10 cups broth. If not, add cans of chicken broth to equal this amount. Bring broth to boil, then simmer until broth is reduced to 5 cups.

• Sauté whole mushrooms and garlic in 2 to 4 tablespoons butter and set aside. In saucepan, melt 3/4 cup butter and stir in flour. Gradually add broth, stirring constantly, until thickened. Add cream and cook until thick and creamy.

• In a lightly greased 3 1/2-quart baking dish, layer half the spaghetti, half the chicken, half the mushrooms, and half the cheese. Pour half the cream sauce over mixture.

• Repeat layers with remaining spaghetti, chicken, mushrooms, and top with Parmesan. Bake at 350° for 30 to 45 minutes.

Chicken Bake

MAKES 5 TO 6 SERVINGS

Did you know the artichoke is an edible thistle? Thistle or not, they are delicious when prepared with chicken.

5 to 6 boneless, skinless chicken breast halves
1/2 cup butter
Paprika
Salt and pepper to taste
2 tablespoons flour
1 pound fresh mushrooms, sliced
14-ounce can chicken broth
1/2 cup sherry
14-ounce can artichoke hearts, drained, quartered

● Sauté chicken in butter and season with paprika, salt, and pepper. Place chicken in one layer in a lightly greased baking dish. Add flour to same skillet and stir constantly to dissolve.

● Stir in mushrooms to sauté and mix well. Add chicken broth and sherry and simmer 5 to 10 minutes, stirring occasionally. Pour broth mixture over chicken and sprinkle with salt and pepper.

● Bake at 350° for 1 hour. Remove from oven and spread artichokes over top. Bake for 20 to 30 minutes more.

Zesty Chicken Bake

MAKES 4 SERVINGS

The cheese livens up this tasty chicken dish.

4 boneless, skinless chicken breasts
1 onion, chopped
2 4-ounce cans chopped green chilies, drained
Oil
2 10 1/2-ounce cans cream of chicken soup
2 5 1/3-ounce cans evaporated milk
10 corn tortillas
8 ounces grated Swiss cheese

● In a saucepan, cook chicken in boiling water until done. Cut into small pieces and set aside.

● In a skillet, cook onion and chilies in oil until tender; drain. Add soup and milk and heat thoroughly. Add chicken.

● Cut tortillas into strips and place in a lightly greased 3-quart casserole. Add chicken and soup mixture; top with cheese. Bake at 325° for 45 minutes.

PREP TIME: 20 MINUTES   COOKING TIME: 40 MINUTES

Artichoke Chicken Casserole

MAKES 2 SERVINGS

Artichokes and chicken—a great combination!

2 boneless, skinless chicken breasts

1 bay leaf

1 cup sherry, divided

Salt and pepper

3 tablespoons butter

1/2 pound fresh mushrooms, sliced

4 green onions with tops, chopped

Garlic salt to taste

2 8 1/2-ounce cans artichoke hearts, drained, quartered

3/4 cup mayonnaise

1/2 cup sour cream

1 cup grated Parmesan cheese, divided

• Boil chicken in water seasoned with bay leaf, half the sherry, salt, and pepper. When chicken is cooked throughout, drain, shred, and put aside.

• In a skillet, melt butter and sauté mushrooms, green onions, and garlic salt. Mix together chicken, artichokes, and mushroom mixture; place in a lightly greased 2-quart baking dish.

• Fold in mayonnaise, sour cream, remaining sherry and 1/2 cup of Parmesan cheese; mix well. Top with remaining Parmesan. Bake uncovered at 350° for 20 minutes.

Chicken Enchiladas

MAKES 6 SERVINGS

This easy enchilada recipe is definitely a keeper!

5 to 6 boneless, skinless chicken breast halves,
  cooked, chopped
Salt
Pepper
Garlic powder
2 cups sour cream
7-ounce can chopped green chilies, drained
16-ounce package shredded Cheddar cheese
16-ounce package shredded Monterey Jack cheese
1 onion, minced
4 10-ounce cans enchilada sauce, divided
10 to 12 corn tortillas, 6 to 8 inches
Vegetable oil

- Lay out chopped chicken on wax paper to season lightly with salt, pepper, and garlic powder. In a mixing bowl, combine sour cream, green chilies, cheeses, and onion. Add chicken and stir to mix.

- In a lightly greased 9 x 13-inch baking dish, spread a portion of the enchilada sauce over the bottom. Dip tortilla in hot oil, drain, and dip in enchilada sauce.

- Spoon some of the chicken mixture into the tortilla. Roll up tortilla and place seam side down on top of enchilada sauce. Repeat with all tortillas.

- Sprinkle enchilada sauce and cheeses over top. Bake at 350° for 30 to 45 minutes.

Poppy Seed Chicken

MAKES 4 SERVINGS

Poppy seeds make for a crunchy, munchie chicken entrée—and it's easy, too!

3 boneless, skinless chicken breasts
1 stalk celery, sliced
1 onion, sliced
Salt and pepper to taste
10 1/2-ounce can cream of chicken soup
1 cup sour cream
1/4 cup white wine
4-ounce can chopped mushrooms, drained
1 cup Ritz crackers, crushed
5 tablespoons butter, melted
3 tablespoons poppy seeds

• Cook chicken in water seasoned with celery, onion, salt, and pepper until tender. Cut up cooked chicken and place in a lightly greased baking dish. Mix soup, sour cream, wine, mushrooms, salt, and pepper and pour over chicken.

• Toast crackers in melted butter. Sprinkle crackers over casserole and top with poppy seeds. Bake at 350° for 30 minutes, uncovered until bubbly.

Chicken Camarillo

MAKES 6 SERVINGS

Classy and easy—that's exactly what this recipe is!

6 boneless, skinless chicken breast halves
3 tablespoons plus 1/4 cup butter
2 avocados, peeled and sliced
1/2 teaspoon grated gingerroot
1/2 cup chicken broth
1/2 cup heavy cream
1 small onion, chopped
1/4 cup crumbled, cooked bacon

• In a skillet, sauté the chicken breasts in 3 tablespoons of butter for about 10 minutes. Remove from heat.

• In a food processor, blend avocados, gingerroot, chicken broth, and cream until smooth. Sauté onion in 1/4 cup butter until golden, then add to avocado mixture.

• Place cooked chicken breasts in a lightly greased baking dish. Pour the avocado mixture over chicken. Top with crumbled bacon. Bake at 400° for 20 minutes.

PREP TIME: 10 MINUTES   COOKING TIME: 45 MINUTES

Creamy Chicken & Ham

MAKES 6 SERVINGS

This is a perfect recipe to use up leftover turkey (instead of chicken) and ham after Thanksgiving or Christmas!

3 tablespoons oil

1 large yellow onion, chopped

1 1/2 cups chopped celery

1 tablespoon minced garlic

1/8 teaspoon ground nutmeg

2 tablespoons flour

2 cups whole milk

2 cups diced, cooked ham

2 cups diced, cooked chicken

14-ounce jar artichoke hearts, cut up, drained

1/2 cup sour cream

1 cup grated Parmesan cheese

12-ounce package penne pasta, cooked, drained

2/3 cup seasoned bread crumbs

• In a large skillet, heat the oil; add onion, celery, garlic, and nutmeg. Cook until onion is softened. Add the flour and cook slowly for about 3 minutes.

• Stir in milk and simmer, stirring constantly until thickened. Fold in ham, chicken, artichoke hearts, sour cream, cheese, and pasta. Mix thoroughly.

• Spoon into a buttered 9 x 13-inch baking dish. Sprinkle crumbs over top of casserole. Bake at 350° for about 30 minutes.

Chicken Linguine

MAKES 4 SERVINGS

A hearty dish that pleases the palate and gets rave reviews!

4 boneless, skinless chicken breasts
1/2 teaspoon salt
1/2 teaspoon pepper
Olive oil
4 green onions and tops, chopped
1/4 cup chopped celery
1 red or yellow bell pepper, cored and chopped
1/2 teaspoon cayenne pepper
1 cup chopped pecans
15-ounce can baby green peas, drained
1/2 cup chicken broth
2/3 cup heavy cream
8 to 10 ounces linguine
1/2 cup Parmesan cheese
parsely, for garnish

• Cut chicken in bite-size pieces and season with salt and pepper. Heat oil in large skillet and add chicken when oil is hot. Cook chicken to golden brown on both sides, lower heat, and cook until tender. Remove chicken from oil, drain, and set aside.

• Sauté onions, celery, and bell pepper in skillet until onions are translucent. Add cayenne pepper and stir to blend. Add pecans, peas, and broth. Stir to combine all ingredients.

• Slowly pour in cream, stirring constantly, and heat until liquid begins to thicken. Remove from heat and continue to stir so sauce won't burn.

• Fill large pot with water and a little salt, and bring to a boil. Add linguine and cook until al dente. Drain linguine and add to cream mixture.

• Add chicken, salt, and white pepper to cream mixture and gently toss to coat linguine and chicken. Place mixture in serving bowl and garnish with fresh Parmesan cheese and parsley.

Coq au Vin

MAKES 6 SERVINGS

This classic French dish moves away from the traditional "white wine with chicken" rule to give the chicken a robust flavor enhancement. Breaking the rules for this dish is well worth it.

5 to 6 pounds boneless, skinless chicken breasts
　and thighs
1/4 to 1/3 cup butter
6 to 8 slices bacon, chopped
1/2 pound mushrooms, sliced
12 to 16 small boiling onions, peeled
2 cloves garlic, minced
2 bay leaves
1 tablespoon thyme
1 tablespoon seasoned salt
1 teaspoon pepper
1/3 cup brandy
4 to 5 cups dry red wine

- Remove all skin and fat from chicken pieces, rinse, and pat dry. In a heavy skillet, melt butter and brown chicken on all sides.

- Cook the bacon at the same time as the chicken and spoon both into a baking dish, undrained. Add to the skillet mushrooms, onions, garlic, bay leaves, thyme, salt, and pepper and sauté until onions and mushrooms are translucent and tender. Spoon over chicken in baking dish.

- Heat brandy in saucepan and pour brandy over the chicken and vegetables. Quickly light with a match and allow the flame to go out. Add 4 cups red wine, cover and bake at 350° for 1 hour or until chicken is tender and cooked throughout. After 30 minutes, check liquid in dish, and add more red wine if needed.

PREP TIME: 25 MINUTES   COOKING TIME: 1 HOUR 50 MINUTES

Orange Baked Quail

MAKES 8 SERVINGS

Oranges add a zesty citrus flavor to this classic quail recipe, and their bright color looks nice in the finished dish.

1 teaspoon seasoned salt

1/2 cup flour

1/4 teaspoon pepper

8 quail, dressed

1/2 cup oil, divided

1/2 onion, chopped

1/2 green bell pepper, chopped

1 clove garlic, minced

1 carrot, sliced

1 cup chicken broth

1 cup white wine

1 tablespoon grated orange rind

1 teaspoon Worcestershire sauce

Sour cream at room temperature

• Mix salt, flour, and pepper in a paper bag. Put quail in bag and shake until lightly coated. In skillet, heat 1/4 cup oil and quickly brown quail over medium-high heat. Put quail in a lightly greased baking dish.

• Sauté onion, bell pepper, and garlic in remaining oil. Add carrot, broth, and wine. Cover and simmer for 15 minutes. Pour over quail and sprinkle with orange rind and Worcestershire sauce.

• Cover and bake at 350° for 45 minutes. Turn off heat and leave in oven an additional 30 minutes. Serve with a dab of sour cream.

Chicken Creole

MAKES 4 SERVINGS

It will look as though you worked all day on this recipe (let them think that), but it's actually very easy to prepare.

1 cup short- or medium-grain rice
1/4 cup butter, melted
3/4 cup chopped, blanched almonds
1/4 cup olive oil
3 tablespoons chopped onions
1 clove garlic, minced
1/2 cup sliced mushrooms
1/4 cup chopped celery
1/4 cup chopped green bell pepper
3 tablespoons flour
1/2 teaspoon salt
1/2 teaspoon pepper
1/4 teaspoon paprika
1/4 teaspoon cayenne
1/2 large tomato, crushed with juice
1 cup chicken broth
2 cups diced, cooked chicken
1/2 cup chopped pimiento, drained
1/4 teaspoon horseradish
1 teaspoon lemon juice
Cayenne pepper to taste
Fresh parsley

• Cook rice according to package directions. Spoon into a lightly greased 7-inch round rice mold or gelatin mold. Drizzle 1/4 cup melted butter over rice.

• Press rice into mold so it will be tight enough to hold its shape. Sprinkle almond pieces over top of rice and pat down lightly. Set mold in pan of water and bake at 350° for 15 to 20 minutes. Remove from oven and set aside.

• In skillet with olive oil, sauté onions and garlic until tender. Add mushrooms, celery, and bell pepper and cook until tender and translucent. Stir in flour, salt, pepper, paprika, and cayenne.

• Add crushed tomato and chicken broth and bring to a boil. Reduce heat and stir in chicken, pimiento, horseradish, lemon juice, and cayenne pepper to taste. Add extra cayenne if desired.

• Simmer for 10 to 15 minutes to blend flavors. Taste for seasonings. Loosen edges of rice mold, invert, and tap the bottom to dislodge rice mold in one piece onto serving platter. Spoon chicken Creole into center of rice ring and garnish with parsley.

Hungarian Cabbage & Chicken

MAKES 6 SERVINGS

$1/4$ cup butter, plus 1 tablespoon for greasing the
  dish

1 fryer chicken, 3 to 4 pounds, cut up

2 teaspoons paprika

1 head cabbage, cut into $1/4$ inch slices

$1/4$ teaspoon salt

$1/4$ teaspoon pepper

2 medium Granny Smith apples, cored and sliced

1 medium onion, chopped

1 tablespoon caraway seeds

2 teaspoons grated lemon rind

1 teaspoon sugar

1 cup shredded Swiss cheese

● Preheat the oven to 350°. Grease a 13 x 9 inch baking dish.

● In a large skillet, heat butter over medium heat until melted. Sprinkle the chicken with paprika and sauté until browned on all sides. Reduce the heat, cover, and simmer for 20 minutes.

● Place the cabbage in the baking dish. Season with salt and pepper, cover, and bake for 20 minutes. Arrange the apples and onion on top of the cabbage and sprinkle with the caraway, lemon rind, and sugar. Top with the chicken pieces, cover, and bake for 30 minutes longer, or until the juices run clear from the chicken and the cabbage is tender. Remove the cover, sprinkle with cheese, and bake for 5 minutes longer.

Rustic Chicken Stew

MAKES 8 SERVINGS

This chunky stew is easy to make and features chicken, carrots, corn, and peas—all tastefully seasoned with thyme.

4 tablespoons olive oil

2 pounds boneless, skinless chicken breasts, cut into 1-inch cubes

3 medium onions, quartered

2 carrots, cut into 1-inch-thick slices

8 ounces mushrooms, halved

2 potatoes, cut into 1-inch cubes

1 cup frozen corn

2 14-ounce cans low-sodium chicken broth

1 teaspoon celery seed

1 teaspoon dried thyme leaves

Salt and freshly ground pepper to taste

1 cup frozen peas

• In a large saucepan or Dutch oven, heat 2 tablespoons oil and cook the chicken, browning on all sides. Set aside. Heat the remaining oil and sauté the onions, carrots, and mushrooms for 5 minutes.

• Stir in the potatoes, chicken, corn, chicken broth, celery seed, thyme, and salt and pepper. Bring to a boil, reduce the heat, and simmer covered for 45 minutes, until the chicken is done and the vegetables are tender. Stir in the peas and cook until they're done.

Turkey Cornbread

MAKES 6 SERVINGS

1 pound ground turkey

1 medium onion, chopped

1 1/2 teaspoons salt

1 teaspoon pepper

1 cup cornmeal

1/2 cup all-purpose flour

1/2 teaspoon baking soda

1 1/2 teaspoons chili powder

2 large eggs, lightly beaten

1 cup buttermilk

1/2 cup canola oil

1 cup canned black-eyed peas, drained

8-ounce can cream-style corn

1 cup shredded cheddar cheese

2 pickled jalapeño peppers, chopped

• Preheat the oven to 325°. In a large skillet over medium heat, sauté the turkey, onion, salt, and pepper for 8 minutes until the turkey is browned and the onion is softened. Drain the liquid from the skillet.

• In a large bowl, mix the cornmeal, flour, baking soda, and chili powder. Add the eggs, buttermilk, and oil, stirring just until the dry ingredients are moistened. Add the meat mixture, peas, corn, cheese, and jalapeños. Transfer into a lightly greased 7 x 11-inch baking dish and bake for 1 hour.

PREP TIME: 25 MINUTES   COOKING TIME: 1 HOUR 20 MINUTES

Louisiana Chicken Gumbo

MAKES 8 SERVINGS

1 tablespoon vegetable oil

2 pounds kielbasa or any smoked pork or beef
  sausage, cut into 1/4-inch-thick slices

8 chicken thighs

8 chicken drumsticks

Salt and pepper, to taste

2 10-ounce boxes frozen whole okra, rinsed and cut
  into 1/2-inch-thick rounds

2 large onions, chopped

3 celery ribs, chopped

8 cups chicken broth

8 cups water

1 bunch thinly sliced scallions, green part only

COOKS' TIP:

Gumbo may be made up to 3 days ahead and refrigerated.

● In a heavy skillet, heat oil over medium-high heat and brown sausage in batches. Drain on paper towels. Season chicken with salt and pepper. Brown chicken pieces in batches in remaining fat. Drain on paper towels.

● Pour off all but 1 tablespoon fat from the skillet and cook okra over medium heat, stirring occasionally, until tender. Add onions and celery, stirring, until vegetables are softened.

● In a Dutch oven, bring broth and water to a boil. Stir in okra mixture and chicken. Reduce the heat and simmer, stirring occasionally for 30 minutes, until chicken is cooked through and liquid has thickened. Add the sausage, scallions, and salt and pepper to taste. Simmer for 5 more minutes. Serve with white rice and Tabasco sauce to add some heat.

PREP TIME: 20 MINUTES   COOKING TIME: 1 HOUR 15 MINUTES

Chicken Posole

MAKES 4 TO 6 SERVINGS

5 cups water

4 chicken breast halves

2 15-ounce cans white hominy, drained

2 14 1/2-ounce cans stewed tomatoes

4 teaspoons dried oregano

1 jalapeño chili, seeded and minced

Dash of hot pepper sauce

Salt and pepper to taste

1 1/2 cups shredded lettuce

1/2 cup sliced radishes

1/4 cup sliced scallions

1 1/2 cups grated Monterey Jack cheese

● In a large saucepan, bring 5 cups of water to a boil. Add chicken, cover, and simmer until cooked through, about 13 minutes. Transfer chicken to a platter to cool slightly, reserving the cooking liquid in the saucepan. Skin and bone the chicken breasts and shred the meat. Set aside.

● Add hominy, tomatoes, oregano, jalapeño, and hot sauce to the reserved cooking liquid. Bring to a boil. Reduce heat and simmer until slightly thickened, stirring often, about 1 hour. Stir in the shredded chicken. Season to taste with salt and pepper and additional hot sauce. (Can be prepared 1 day ahead up until this point. Cover and refrigerate. Bring to simmer before serving.)

● Divide the lettuce, radishes, and scallions equally among soup bowls. Ladle the posole into the bowls and top with the shredded cheese.

Savory Meals with Meat

Lamb & Eggplant Casserole •
Lamb & Artichoke Stew •
Apple-Raisin Stuffed Chops •
Baked Spaghetti •
Spaghetti Casserole •
Stromboli Hero •
Beef Burritos •
Company Beef & Pasta •
Beef à la Bourguignonne •
Mexican Casserole •
Beef & Broccoli Pasta •
Oven Steak •
Moussaka •
Sunday Night Cheesy-Beefy Casserole •
Beef-Noodle Casserole •
Stuffed Manicotti •

• Beef Pappardelle
• Beef Stew
• Cheesy Stuffed Bell Peppers
• Veal Steak Casserole
• Spicy Lasagna
• Ham & Asparagus Casserole
• Sweet and Sour Cabbage Rolls
• Company Beef Casserole
• Baked Veal
• Ham and Black Bean Soup with Chilies
• Comfort Casserole
• Veal, Peppers & Pasta
• Ham Loaf
• Beef en Cocotte
• Hearty Kielbasa Soup

PREP TIME: 15 MINUTES   COOKING TIME: 40 MINUTES

Lamb & Eggplant Casserole

MAKES 4 SERVINGS

Lamb and eggplant make for a nice change of pace from chicken and beef.

1 *pound ground lamb*

1 *large eggplant*

1 *large tomato, chopped*

1/2 cup chopped green onions with tops

1*1/2 teaspoons salt*

1/2 teaspoon curry powder

1/2 teaspoon paprika

4 *tablespoons snipped parsley*

- Brown ground lamb in skillet, drain on paper towels, and set aside to cool. Peel and finely chop the eggplant.

- Combine lamb, eggplant, tomato, onions, salt, curry powder, paprika, and parsley, and stir to mix thoroughly.

- Spoon the mixture into a lightly greased baking dish and spread evenly in dish. Bake at 350° for 30 to 40 minutes until top is brown.

Lamb & Artichoke Stew

MAKES 6 SERVINGS

2 *lemons*

8 *whole fresh artichokes*

1/4 *cup extra-virgin olive oil*

1 *medium yellow onion, minced*

4 *green onions*

1 1/2 *pounds boneless leg of lamb steaks cut into 1-inch cubes*

1 *cup plus 2 tablespoons beef or lamb stock*

salt and freshly ground black pepper

1 *egg, plus 1 egg yolk*

1 1/2 *teaspoons cornstarch*

● Fill a bowl of water and add the slices of one lemon. Slice the artichokes in half and place them in the lemon water to prevent discoloration.

● Pour the oil into a large saucepan, and over medium heat, sauté the onion until translucent, about 5 minutes. Add the green onions and cook for 3 to 4 minutes.

● Raise the heat to high and add the lamb. Sauté the meat until it browns on all sides. Add stock and salt and pepper. When it comes to a boil, lower the heat, cover, and simmer for 15 to 20 minutes. Remove the pan from the heat.

● In a large bowl, whisk together the egg, yolk, juice of one lemon, 2 tablespoons stock, and cornstarch. Slowly ladle the hot stock into the cornstarch mixture to temper the eggs, ensuring that they won't scramble. When all the hot stock is incorporated, pour the egg mixture back into the saucepan. Toss to coat the lamb and add the artichoke halves. Let stand until the sauce thickens, about 2 minutes. Serve warm.

PREP TIME: 40 MINUTES   COOKING TIME: 1 HOUR 35 MINUTES

Apple-Raisin Stuffed Chops

MAKES 6 SERVINGS

3/4 cup dried apples

1 cup apple juice

1/2 cup seedless raisins

1/2 cup walnuts

2 tablespoons fine dry bread crumbs

1 tablespoon sugar

2 tablespoons dry white wine

1 tablespoon lemon juice

1/2 teaspoon ground ginger

6 pork loin chops, cut 1-inch thick

2 tablespoons vegetable oil

salt and freshly ground black pepper

● Preheat the oven to 350°.

● Combine in a saucepan the apples and apple juice. Simmer covered for 25 minutes. Remove from the heat. Add the raisins and let stand 5 minutes; drain, reserving the liquid.

● Combine the cooked fruit, walnuts, and bread crumbs. In a small bowl, stir together the sugar, wine, lemon juice, and ginger. Add to the bread mixture, tossing lightly to moisten.

● Cut pockets in the side of the chops, through the fatty side, lengthwise to the bone. Spoon about 1/3 cup of the stuffing mixture into the side pocket. Repeat with remaining chops. If necessary, use wooden picks to hold pockets closed.

● In a large skillet, heat the oil and brown the chops on both sides.

● Place the chops in a lightly greased 9 x 13-inch baking pan.

● Season the chops with salt and pepper. Add 1/4 cup reserved apple liquid to the pan, adding more water if necessary. Bake the chops, covered, for 1 hour.

PREP TIME: 15 MINUTES (REFRIGERATE 2 HOURS)   COOKING TIME: 1 HOUR

Baked Spaghetti

MAKES 6 SERVINGS

Prepare this dish in the morning when you are fresh and energetic (hopefully), and supper will be ready to bake when you get home.

8 ounces spaghetti

1 pound ground beef

1 green bell pepper, chopped

1 onion, chopped

10 1/2-ounce can tomato bisque soup

15-ounce can tomato sauce

2/3 cup water

1/2 teaspoon salt

2 teaspoons Italian seasoning

8-ounce can whole kernel corn, drained

4-ounce can sliced black olives, drained

8-ounce package shredded Cheddar cheese

● Cook spaghetti as package directs, drain, and set aside. In skillet, cook beef, bell pepper, and onion; drain. Add remaining ingredients and spaghetti to beef mixture and stir.

● Pour into a greased 9 x 13-inch baking dish and cover. Refrigerate two to three hours. Bake covered at 350° for 45 minutes.

PREP TIME: 30 MINUTES   COOKING TIME: 1 HOUR

Spaghetti Casserole

MAKES 6 SERVINGS

You will have requests for this recipe on family dinner night.

2 tablespoons butter

1 clove garlic

1 teaspoon sugar

1 teaspoon salt

1/4 teaspoon pepper

1 1/2 pounds ground beef

2 8-ounce cans tomato sauce

8-ounce package spaghetti

3-ounce package cream cheese, softened

1 1/2 cups sour cream

5 green onions with tops, chopped

8 ounces grated Cheddar cheese

● In a skillet, melt butter with garlic, sugar, salt, and pepper. Cook until butter is melted, then add meat and brown. Add tomato sauce and simmer, uncovered, for 20 minutes.

● Cook spaghetti according to package directions; drain. Place spaghetti in a lightly greased 9 x 13-inch baking dish.

● Mix together cream cheese, sour cream, and green onions, and pour over spaghetti. Add meat mixture and top with Cheddar cheese. Bake uncovered at 350° for 30 minutes.

Stromboli Hero

MAKES 4 SERVINGS

News flash! A loaf of bread filled with meat and cheese—what more could you ask for?

3/4 pound ground beef
Salt
Pepper
1 pound ground pork sausage
1/2 teaspoon rosemary
2 cloves garlic, minced
1/2 cup grated Parmesan cheese
15-ounce can tomato sauce
1 loaf French bread
8-ounce package mozzarella cheese

- Season ground beef with salt and pepper. Brown in skillet with pork sausage until crumbly. Stir in rosemary, garlic, Parmesan, and tomato sauce, and simmer to reduce liquid.

- Cut French bread in half horizontally; hollow out bread from inside, leaving crust of 1/4 to 1/2-inch. Sprinkle half the mozzarella in shell, then all the meat mixture, then the remaining mozzarella.

- Replace horizontal top on bread shell. Wrap in foil and place in a 9 x 13-inch baking dish. Bake at 350° for 10 to 15 minutes or until thoroughly heated.

PREP TIME: 15 MINUTES   COOKING TIME: 45 MINUTES

Beef Burritos

MAKES 6 SERVINGS

This is an easy dish that can be made in advance, then popped in the oven when you're ready to eat. Serve it with chips, salsa, a green salad, or guacamole on lettuce.

1 pound ground beef
1 onion, diced
1 to 2 tablespoons oil
4-ounce can chopped green chilies, drained
1 tablespoon salt
1 teaspoon pepper
1/2 teaspoon garlic powder
1/2 teaspoon cayenne pepper (optional)
15-ounce can refried beans
12 flour tortillas
1 cup grated Cheddar cheese

• Brown ground beef in large skillet and pour off excess fat. Add onion to meat and sauté until onion is translucent and tender. Add 1 to 2 tablespoons of oil and stir in green chilies and seasonings.

• Cook 3 to 4 minutes to blend ingredients. Stir in refried beans and cook several minutes until well blended.

• Scoop 3 to 4 tablespoons of meat mixture into each tortilla and sprinkle cheese over top. Roll up tortilla and fold ends toward the center just before the last roll.

• Place in a prepared 9 x 13-inch baking dish, seam side down. Cover and bake at 350° for 20 to 25 minutes or until heated throughout.

Company Beef & Pasta

MAKES 6 SERVINGS

This recipe will serve a bunch and tastes much better than the usual "beef and potato" fare. Just add a tossed salad and Italian bread.

2 pounds lean, ground round beef

2 onions, chopped

1 green bell pepper, chopped

1/2 teaspoon garlic powder

14-ounce jar spaghetti sauce

15-ounce can Italian stewed tomatoes

4-ounce can sliced mushrooms, drained

8-ounce package rotini pasta

1 1/2 pints sour cream, divided

8 ounces provolone cheese, sliced

8-ounce package shredded mozzarella cheese

• In a deep skillet or kettle, brown and cook beef, stirring often with a fork. Drain off excess fat. Add onions, bell pepper, garlic powder, spaghetti sauce, stewed tomatoes, and mushrooms. Mix well. Simmer 20 minutes.

• Cook rotini according to package directions; drain. Pour half the rotini into a large, deep, buttered casserole dish. Cover with half the meat-tomato mixture and half the sour cream. Top with slices of provolone cheese. Repeat process once more, ending with the mozzarella cheese in place of the provolone.

• Cover and bake at 350° for 35 minutes. Remove cover and continue baking another 10 to 15 minutes or until mozzarella cheese melts.

PREP TIME: 15 MINUTES   COOK TIME: 3 HOURS 40 MINUTES

Beef à la Bourguignonne

MAKES 6 SERVINGS

This hearty beef dish cooked in its own juices with burgundy wine, mushrooms, and baby onions will make everyone glad they know you.

3 *to 4 pounds beef chuck or round steak, cut into*
  3/4-inch cubes
2 *tablespoons oil*
3 *tablespoons flour*
3/4 *teaspoon seasoned salt*
1/2 *teaspoon pepper*
1/2 *teaspoon thyme*
1/4 *teaspoon garlic powder*
14-*ounce can beef broth*
1 *cup burgundy wine*
11/2 *cups sliced fresh mushrooms*
2 15-*ounce cans small white onions, drained*
Cooked white rice

● In a large skillet, brown meat in 2 tablespoons oil. Add flour, salt, pepper, thyme, and garlic powder. Place in a 3-quart baking dish. Add beef broth and wine; stir well.

● Cover and bake for 2 hours. Add mushrooms and onions and bake for another 1 hour and 30 minutes. If meat becomes too dry, add equal portions of wine and water. Serve over white rice.

PREP TIME: 15 MINUTES   COOKING TIME: 1 HOUR

Mexican Casserole

MAKES 6 SERVINGS

This is supper: well seasoned, well done, and soon gone.

1¹/2 pounds ground round

1 teaspoon seasoned salt

1 large onion, chopped

1 red bell pepper, chopped

1 yellow bell pepper, chopped

3 cups chopped zucchini

1/2 to ³/4 cup water

1 envelope taco seasoning

1 cup uncooked rice

12-ounce jar chunky salsa

1¹/2 cups grated Cheddar cheese

³/4 to 1 cup crumbled tortilla chips

● Brown the ground round with seasoned salt, then add onion, bell peppers, zucchini, water, and taco seasoning. Stir and sauté until vegetables are tender.

● In separate saucepan, cook rice according to directions. In a lightly greased 9 x 13-inch baking dish, spoon rice over bottom of dish, then add layer of beef mixture, salsa, and cheese.

● Bake at 350° for 20 to 25 minutes. Remove from oven and sprinkle tortilla chips over top. Bake for another 10 minutes.

PREP TIME: 35 MINUTES   COOKING TIME: 55 MINUTES

Beef & Broccoli Pasta

MAKES 6 SERVINGS

Adding broccoli to this classic Italian recipe dresses it up and adds wonderful flavor.

6 ounces uncooked fettuccine

3/4 pound ground round or beef chuck

1 clove garlic, minced

1 onion, minced

8-ounces tomato sauce

15-ounce can stewed Italian tomatoes, undrained

1/2 teaspoon Italian seasoning

2 eggs, divided

2 tablespoons butter

8-ounce package shredded mozzarella cheese

8-ounce carton small-curd cottage cheese, drained

1 cup chopped fresh broccoli

1/3 cup grated fresh Parmesan cheese

• Cook fettuccine as directed, drain, and set aside. In a large skillet, brown beef and stir to crumble. Add garlic and onion, stir to mix, and reduce heat. Drain excess grease.

• Add tomato sauce, stewed tomatoes with liquid, and Italian seasoning. Stir and bring to a boil. Reduce heat, cover, and simmer for 10 to 12 minutes, stirring occasionally.

• Beat 1 egg and melted butter in mixing bowl. Stir in fettuccine and mozzarella cheese. Spoon mixture into ungreased 9-inch pie plate and press down on bottom and sides of plate to compact fettuccine mixture.

• Mix remaining egg and the cottage cheese in a separate bowl. Pour over fettuccine in pie plate and smooth over surface. Sprinkle with broccoli. Spoon beef mixture evenly over top.

• Sprinkle Parmesan evenly over top and remove any cheese from edges of pie plate. Bake at 350° for 30 minutes or until hot throughout. Let stand 5 to 10 minutes to set before cutting.

Oven Steak

MAKES 6 TO 8 SERVINGS

Well-prepared steak makes a savory and satisfying centerpiece for both formal and casual meals.

2 pounds of 1¹/2-inch-thick round steak

1 teaspoon garlic salt

1 teaspoon seasoned salt

¹/2 teaspoon black pepper

¹/2 cup flour

¹/4 cup oil

28-ounce can tomatoes, undrained

1 green bell pepper, seeded, cored, and sliced in
  rings

1 small yellow onion, sliced in rings

● Remove excess fat from round steak and cut into 6 to 8 individual steaks. In a bowl, combine garlic salt, seasoned salt, pepper, and flour. Coat steaks with flour mixture.

● In skillet, heat oil until hot. Brown steak on both sides, remove from pan, and place in a lightly greased baking dish.

● In a blender, process tomatoes until puréed. Pour tomatoes over steak and top with peppers and onion. Bake covered at 325° for 2 to 3 hours, depending on desired doneness.

Moussaka

MAKES 6 SERVINGS

This is an old-time recipe and takes a little more preparation, but it's well worth it.

1/2 cup olive oil, divided

3 cloves garlic, minced

1 onion, chopped

1 1/2 pounds ground round or chuck

2 teaspoons basil

1 teaspoon oregano

1/2 teaspoon cinnamon

1/2 teaspoon seasoned salt

1/2 teaspoon pepper

2 8-ounce cans tomato sauce

2 pounds eggplant

Salt

2 baking potatoes

3 eggs

2 tablespoons flour

2 cups plain yogurt or sour cream

1/2 to 3/4 cup grated Parmesan cheese

- To make meat sauce, heat 2 tablespoons oil in large skillet and sauté garlic and onion until onion is translucent. Add ground meat, brown, and reduce heat to cook until meat is no longer pink. Drain and return to skillet.

- Add basil, oregano, cinnamon, seasoned salt, pepper, and tomato sauce. Increase heat to boiling, then reduce heat to low and simmer for 15 minutes, stirring occasionally. Set aside.

- To make eggplant mixture, cut eggplant into thick slices, salt both sides, and place in colander. Set aside for 15 to 20 minutes. Peel potatoes and slice thinly. In a saucepan, cover potatoes with water, bring to a boil, and reduce heat to simmer until potatoes are fork tender. Drain and set aside.

- After beads of liquid form on the eggplant, use a paper towel to pat dry. Brush with olive oil and place under broiler for 3 to 4 minutes per side or until both sides are golden brown.

- To make topping, beat eggs and gradually add flour while beating. Add yogurt and mix thoroughly. Make sure mixture is smooth without any lumps.

- Place some of the eggplant and potato slices in one layer on bottom of a lightly greased 9 x 13-inch baking dish. Spoon half the meat mixture evenly over the eggplant and potato slices.

- Repeat layers using all the eggplant and potato slices. Spoon yogurt sauce over top and spread to smooth. Sprinkle with cheese and bake at 375° for 40 to 45 minutes or until bubbly and golden brown.

Sunday Night Cheesy-Beefy Casserole

MAKES 4 SERVINGS

Make this well-seasoned beef casserole on Saturday morning and it will be ready for Sunday night after a busy day off.

1 pound ground beef

1 large onion, chopped

1 cup chopped green bell pepper

1/3 cup water

1 1/2 teaspoons sugar

1 tablespoon chili powder

2 teaspoons ground cumin

1/2 teaspoon dried oregano

14 1/2-ounce can diced tomatoes, undrained

4 1/2-ounce can chopped green chilies, drained

3 cups cooked long-grain rice

1 cup sour cream

1/4 cup milk

1 cup grated sharp Cheddar cheese

• Cook ground beef, onion, and bell pepper in a large, nonstick skillet over medium-high heat until meat is browned; stir to crumble.

• Add water, sugar, seasonings, tomatoes, and chilies. Bring to a boil. Cover, reduce heat, and simmer 15 minutes. Uncover and simmer an additional 2 minutes to reduce liquid. Remove from heat; set aside.

• In a medium bowl, combine the rice, sour cream, and milk. Lightly grease a 9-inch baking dish and spoon rice mixture into the dish.

• Top with beef mixture; sprinkle with cheese. Bake at 375° for 10 minutes or until thoroughly heated. Let stand 5 minutes before serving.

PREP TIME: 10 MINUTES   COOKING TIME: 35 MINUTES

Beef-Noodle Casserole

MAKES 4 SERVINGS

Here's family fare in a stick-to-the-ribs casserole.

3 tablespoons butter

1 1/2 pounds ground round

1/3 cup sliced scallions

2 8-ounce cans tomato sauce

Dash of Worcestershire sauce

8 ounce package cream cheese, softened

1/2 cup sour cream

1 cup cottage cheese

8 ounces noodles, cooked, drained

- In a skillet, melt 1 tablespoon of butter. Brown beef until crumbly. Add scallions, tomato sauce, and Worcestershire sauce, and mix.

- In a bowl combine cream cheese, sour cream, and cottage cheese. Place half the noodles in a lightly greased 2-quart baking dish.

- Add the cheese mixture and put remaining noodles on top of cheeses. Top with beef mixture. Bake at 350° for 20 minutes.

Stuffed Manicotti

MAKES 6 SERVINGS

Always a delightful dish; just let the manicotti shells cool before trying to "stuff"—you don't want burned fingers.

2 pounds ground round or chuck

3 cloves garlic, minced

1 bell pepper, chopped

1 onion, chopped

6-ounce can tomato paste

2 16-ounce cans tomato sauce

1 1/2 teaspoons sugar

2 tablespoons snipped sweet basil

Salt to taste

Pepper to taste

1 cup water

2 cups grated mozzarella cheese

16-ounce carton ricotta cheese

8-ounce package manicotti shells, cooked, drained

1 1/2 cups grated Parmesan cheese

• Brown ground meat with garlic, bell pepper, and onion, and drain thoroughly. To make sauce, stir in tomato paste, tomato sauce, sugar, basil, salt, pepper, and water. Simmer for 30 to 45 minutes, stirring occasionally.

• Pour 1/2 cup sauce to cover the bottom of a lightly greased 9 x 13-inch baking dish. In a separate bowl, combine mozzarella and ricotta.

• Stuff manicotti shells with cheeses and lay on top of sauce. Pour remaining sauce over shells and sprinkle with Parmesan. Bake at 350° for about 30 minutes.

Beef Pappardelle

MAKES 4 SERVINGS

Ground beef at its best!

8-ounce package pappardelle, radiatore, ricciolini,
   or rigatoni noodles

1 pound ground chuck or round beef

2 cloves garlic, minced

1/2 teaspoon pepper

1 teaspoon seasoned salt

6-ounce can tomato paste

3 cups water

1 1/2-ounce envelope spaghetti sauce mix

1/2 teaspoon crushed dried thyme

3-ounce package cream cheese, softened

8-ounce carton sour cream

3/4 cup grated Parmesan cheese, divided

2 tablespoons snipped parsley

• In a large saucepan filled with water, cook noodles according to package directions. Drain and set aside.

• In a skillet, brown ground chuck until crumbly and cooked throughout. Stir in garlic and sauté until tender and translucent. Drain beef in skillet, season with pepper and seasoned salt, and stir to mix. Set aside.

• In a mixing bowl, combine tomato paste, water, spaghetti sauce mix, and thyme. Stir to mix thoroughly. Pour tomato sauce into beef mixture, bring to a boil, and reduce heat to simmer for 20 to 25 minutes.

• In a lightly greased 3-quart baking dish, spread half the cooked noodles over the bottom. Spoon half the tomato sauce and beef mixture over noodles.

• In a separate bowl, combine cream cheese, sour cream, 1/3 cup Parmesan, and parsley. Stir to mix. Spoon half the cream cheese over tomato sauce and beef mixture.

• Layer remaining noodles on top, then remaining tomato sauce and beef mixture and then a final layer of cream cheese.

• Sprinkle with remaining Parmesan cheese and bake at 350° for 15 to 20 minutes, or until heated throughout.

Beef Stew

MAKES 4 SERVINGS

This is the ultimate slow-cooked meal. Put this recipe together in the morning, then run home at lunch (make any excuse you can), place in oven, and supper is ready at 6. It just takes a little planning.

2 pounds stew meat, cut in bite-size pieces

1 cup sliced carrots

1 onion, chopped

4 potatoes, peeled, cubed

1 cup chopped celery

2 teaspoons salt

1 teaspoon pepper

$10^{1}/_{2}$-ounce can cream of mushroom soup

$^{1}/_{2}$ cup water

1 dried bay leaf, crumbled

$^{1}/_{2}$ cup burgundy wine

- Mix all ingredients in a lightly greased baking dish. Bake at 275° for 5 hours.

Cheesy Stuffed Bell Peppers

MAKES 6 SERVINGS

Stuffed peppers have to be a "down-home" special supper! In just about every casserole we make, we use bell peppers, but with this recipe you get the whole pepper with just the right "stuff" to make it delicious.

6 green bell peppers
1 1/4 pounds lean ground beef
1/2 cup chopped onion
3/4 cup cooked rice
1 egg
2 15-ounce cans Italian stewed tomatoes
1 tablespoon Worcestershire sauce
1/2 teaspoon seasoned salt
1/2 teaspoon black pepper
1/2 teaspoon garlic powder
2 cups shredded Cheddar cheese

• Cut off a small portion of the tops of the bell peppers; remove seeds and membranes. Place in a roaster with salted water and bring to a boil. Cook 10 minutes (they will not be completely done). Drain and set aside to cool.

• In a skillet, brown the ground beef and onion; drain. Add rice, egg, 1 can tomatoes, Worcestershire sauce, and seasonings. Simmer 5 minutes. Remove from heat and add 1 cup cheese, mixing well.

• Stuff the peppers with the mixture and set upright in a buttered, round baking dish. (You may have to trim little slivers off the bottoms of the peppers so they will sit upright.) Pour the remaining can of tomatoes on and around the peppers.

• Bake uncovered at 350° for 25 minutes. Remove from oven and sprinkle remaining cheese on top and return to oven for 10 minutes.

PREP TIME: 10 MINUTES   COOKING TIME: 40 MINUTES

Veal Steak Casserole

MAKES 8 SERVINGS

This recipe makes a creamy sauce (you could call it gravy) that tastes wonderful spooned over a hot biscuit or roll.

1 to 1 1/2 pounds thin veal steak
1/4 to 1/2 cup flour
3 to 4 tablespoons olive oil, divided
1/3 cup chili sauce
2 medium onions, sliced
10 1/2-ounce can beef broth
1 teaspoon salt
2 cups uncooked noodles
10 1/2-ounce can condensed cream of chicken soup
1/2 cup seasoned bread crumbs
2 tablespoons melted butter
1/4 to 1/2 cup grated Parmesan cheese
Parsley to garnish
Green onions with tops to garnish

• Place veal in flour and pat to coat both sides. Cut in bite-size pieces and drop in flour and coat again. Brown both sides of veal in skillet with 2 to 3 tablespoons olive oil.

• Reduce heat to low and add chili sauce, onions, and beef broth. Cover and simmer about 30 minutes, stirring occasionally.

• Fill large saucepan with about 5 to 6 cups water and bring to boil. Add salt and 1 tablespoon olive oil to water and slowly add pasta. Cook pasta until al dente by tasting pasta as it cooks.

• When there is no taste of raw flour and the pasta still maintains some resistance to the bite, remove saucepan from heat, and with a pasta scoop, let pasta drip-dry for a few seconds over the saucepan before dropping into a buttered mixing bowl.

• Toss pasta with cream of chicken soup. Toss well to thoroughly coat pasta. Pour into serving bowl and spoon veal mixture around the edges of the bowl.

• In the center, on top of the pasta, sprinkle seasoned bread crumbs and drizzle melted butter. Top with grated Parmesan cheese. Garnish with parsley and green onions.

PREP TIME: 30 MINUTES   COOKING TIME: 1 HOUR

Spicy Lasagna

MAKES 6 SERVINGS

The spicy sausage takes traditional lasagna to the next level.

1 pound hot Italian sausage

8-ounce package hot pork sausage

1 onion, chopped

3 cloves garlic, minced

2 tablespoons oil

28-ounce can crushed tomatoes

6-ounce can tomato paste

1 1/2 teaspoons basil

1 1/2 teaspoons oregano

1/2 teaspoon salt

1 cup grated Parmesan cheese

2 cups small-curd cottage cheese, drained

1 egg, beaten

1 cup fresh parsley, snipped, divided

6 lasagna noodles, cooked

12-ounce package shredded mozzarella cheese

• Brown both sausages in large skillet until crumbly and no longer pink. Drain through strainer and remove grease from skillet. Sauté onion and garlic with oil in skillet. Cook until translucent and stir to keep from burning.

• Add crushed tomatoes, tomato paste, and seasonings, and stir to mix. Allow to cook until liquid has thickened enough to be spooned out of skillet and spread easily over noodles. Add sausage to the tomato mixture and stir to mix.

• In a separate bowl, add Parmesan, cottage cheese, egg, and half the parsley. Stir to mix. In a lightly greased 9 x 13-inch baking dish, spoon a thin layer of sausage-tomato mixture over the bottom of the dish.

• Layer half the noodles, half the Parmesan mixture, half the mozzarella, and half the sausage-tomato mixture. Repeat the layers using the remaining noodles, Parmesan mixture, mozzarella, and sausage-tomato mixture.

• Sprinkle the top with remaining parsley. Cover with foil and bake at 350° for 30 to 35 minutes until bubbly.

Ham & Asparagus Casserole

MAKES 4 SERVINGS

This beautiful dish is a great way to use up small chunks of leftover ham.

4 eggs
4-ounce package almond slivers or almond slices
2 tablespoons butter, plus extra for topping
1/2 cup seasoned bread crumbs, plus extra for topping
1 pound fresh asparagus, trimmed
2 cups cooked, cubed ham
1/2 cup grated Cheddar cheese
3 tablespoons tapioca
3 tablespoons chopped green onions with tops
1/4 cup chopped mushrooms
3 tablespoons minced red bell pepper
2 tablespoons fresh, snipped parsley
1 tablespoon lemon juice
1/2 cup milk
10 1/2-ounce can of cream of mushroom soup
Paprika

● In a saucepan, cover eggs with water. Cook until hard-boiled, about 12 to 15 minutes. Remove from heat, drain, and set aside to cool.

● Pour almond slivers onto baking sheet and toast at 250° for 10 to 15 minutes. Remove and set aside to cool.

● In a saucepan, melt butter and remove from heat. Add bread crumbs and toss to coat. Set aside. Arrange fresh asparagus in steamer basket and cook in saucepan of water for about 2 to 3 minutes until slightly tender. Drain, arrange asparagus in a lightly greased 1 1/2-quart baking dish, and set aside.

● In a mixing bowl, stir together ham, Cheddar cheese, tapioca, onions, mushrooms, almonds, bell pepper, parsley, and lemon juice until well mixed.

● Remove shells from eggs and carefully make thin slices diagonally across eggs. If eggs are still warm and hard to cut, put in refrigerator to chill. Spoon a layer of half the ham mixture over asparagus and top with a layer of half the egg slices. Repeat layers with remaining ham mixture and egg slices.

● In mixing bowl pour milk into mushroom soup and whisk until well blended. Slowly pour over ham mixture in baking dish. Top with bread crumbs and small sprinkles of paprika. Bake at 350° for 25 to 30 minutes.

Sweet and Sour Cabbage Rolls

MAKES 6 SERVINGS

This handcrafted casserole dish is fun to make and tastes wonderful. Best of all, it tastes even better on the second day.

1/4 cup olive oil

1/2 cup minced onion

1/2 cup minced celery

4 cloves garlic, minced

2 28-ounce cans crushed tomatoes

1 tablespoon tomato paste

1/4 cup dry red wine

1/4 cup minced fresh parsley

2 tablespoons minced fresh basil

1 tablespoon oregano

1/2 teaspoon nutmeg

2 teaspoons salt, divided

1 1/2 teaspoon black pepper, divided

1/4 teaspoon cayenne

1 head green cabbage

15-ounce can stewed tomatoes

1 cup water

1 tablespoon lemon juice

1/4 cup packed brown sugar

1 teaspoon ground ginger

3/4 cup cooked white rice

8 ounces ground pork sausage

1 pound ground chuck roast

1/2 cup chopped green onions with tops

1/2 teaspoon thyme

1 teaspoon caraway seeds

1 1/2 cups sauerkraut, rinsed and drained

Fresh parsley

● In heavy saucepan, heat oil and sauté onion, celery, and garlic. Cook until ingredients are tender and translucent. Over medium heat, pour in crushed tomatoes, tomato paste, red wine, minced parsley, basil, oregano, nutmeg, 1 teaspoon salt, 1/2 teaspoon pepper, and cayenne. Cook for 10 to 15 minutes, stirring occasionally.

● Tear off 8 to 10 large whole cabbage leaves and wash. Fill large pot at least half full of water and bring to a boil. Submerge cabbage leaves in boiling water, one at a time, and cook for 5 minutes or until tender. Remove from pot and dunk in a bowl of cold water to cool, then drain and set aside.

● To heavy saucepan containing tomato sauce mixture, add stewed tomatoes, water, lemon juice, brown sugar, and ginger. Stir to mix and set aside.

• In separate bowl, mix together rice, pork, beef, green onions, thyme, caraway seeds, 1 teaspoon salt, and 1 teaspoon pepper. Stir to mix well. In a lightly greased baking dish, spread 1 cup sauerkraut over bottom of dish and set aside.

• On large cutting board surface or counter, spread out several whole cabbage leaves. Spoon about 1/3 to 1/2 cup meat filling into center of cabbage leaf. Fold one side over filling, then fold in both ends. Roll tightly to hold ends in place. Place seam side down in baking dish with sauerkraut.

• Repeat process with each cabbage leaf until meat mixture is gone. Arrange cabbage rolls in one layer on top of sauerkraut, then add remaining sauerkraut.

• Bring tomato sauce mixture to a boil and pour over sauerkraut and cabbage rolls. Cover with aluminum foil and bake at 350° for 1 hour and 45 minutes. Garnish with fresh parsley and serve.

Company Beef Casserole

MAKES 6 SERVINGS

This is an everyday family meal made special by the rich tastes of the cream cheese, sour cream, and Cheddar cheese.

2 pounds lean, ground round steak

1 teaspoon seasoned salt

1 tablespoon sugar

1/2 teaspoon black pepper

2 15-ounce cans stewed tomatoes

2 8-ounce cans tomato sauce

3 cloves garlic, finely minced

8-ounce package angel hair pasta

8-ounce package cream cheese

1 pint sour cream

2 bunches fresh green onions with tops, chopped

8-ounce package shredded Cheddar cheese

- In a roaster or large skillet, brown ground beef. Drain. Add seasonings, tomatoes, tomato sauce, and garlic; simmer 10 minutes.

- Cook pasta as directed on package; drain. Add cream cheese and stir until cream cheese has melted. Add sour cream and green onions.

- In a 9 x 13-inch buttered baking dish, layer the pasta and meat mixture and top with shredded cheese.

- Bake covered at 325° for 30 minutes. Uncover and bake for another 15 minutes.

Baked Veal

MAKES 4 SERVINGS

This casserole is loaded with tasty ingredients, which makes this veal dish top-notch.

2 1/2 *pounds veal*

1/2 *cup flour*

2 *teaspoons paprika*

2 *teaspoons salt*

1 *teaspoon pepper*

1/2 *cup butter*

2 *cloves garlic, minced*

1 1/2 *cups water*

1 *beef bouillon cube*

2 *cups sour cream*

2 *cups sliced water chestnuts, drained*

1 *teaspoon basil*

1/8 *teaspoon rosemary*

1 *teaspoon lemon juice*

1/4 *cup dry sherry*

• With a meat mallet, pound veal thin and cut into strips. Dip veal into a mixture of flour, paprika, salt, and pepper.

• In a skillet, heat butter and garlic. Brown veal, adding more butter if necessary. Remove veal and garlic from skillet and discard garlic. Add water and bouillon cube to skillet and stir until dissolved.

• Add sour cream, lower heat, and mix thoroughly. Add veal, water chestnuts, and remaining ingredients and stir. Pour into a lightly greased baking dish and bake at 350°, covered, for 1 hour. Serve with rice.

PREP TIME: 15 MINUTES   COOKING TIME: 1 HOUR

Ham and Black Bean Soup with Chilies

MAKES 6 SERVINGS

Shredded carrots add a splash of color to this peppery soup.

2 *tablespoons vegetable oil*

1/2 *pound ham, finely chopped*

2 *medium onions, chopped*

2 *medium-hot chili peppers (such as jalapeño, serrano, or poblano), finely chopped*

1 *large green bell pepper, chopped*

2 *carrots, chopped*

2 *14-ounce cans of beef broth*

15-ounce can of black beans, rinsed and drained

1 *bay leaf*

1/2 *teaspoon cumin seeds*

freshly ground black pepper to taste

● In a large saucepan or Dutch oven, heat the oil over medium-high heat. Brown the ham about 5 minutes. Add the onions, chili peppers, bell peppers, and carrots, sautéing until softened, about 8 minutes.

● Pour in the broth, beans, bay leaf, cumin, and black pepper. Bring to a boil, and then reduce to a simmer. Cook covered for 50 minutes, or until vegetables are tender and flavors have melded.

COOKS' TIP:

If you prefer a less spicy soup, use only 1 medium-hot chili or substitute a mild variety, such as Anaheim.

Comfort Casserole

MAKES 6 SERVINGS

Spaghetti sauce on noodles! Let's be creative—you don't have to have a cream sauce on noodles.

Oil

Salt

6 cups egg noodles, uncooked, divided

3 tablespoons butter, melted

1 1/2 pounds ground chuck or ground round, divided

2 1/2 cups spaghetti sauce, divided

12-ounce package shredded mozzarella cheese

- Add a drop or two of oil to water with a dash of salt and cook noodles as package directs. Drain thoroughly and coat with butter.

- Brown ground chuck and drain thoroughly. Pour half of the spaghetti sauce in the bottom of a lightly greased 9 x 13-inch baking dish. Add half the noodles, half the meat, and half the cheese. Repeat for second layer.

- Bake covered at 300° until cheese melts and dish is heated throughout.

PREP TIME: 15 MINUTES   COOKING TIME: 55 MINUTES

Veal, Peppers & Pasta

MAKES 6 SERVINGS

Sweet red bell pepper and bright green peas make a colorful as well as a delicious casserole. The combination of ingredients in this dish gives it variety and substance, as well as flavor.

8-ounce package linguine
1 pound veal cutlets, sliced into strips
1 sweet red bell pepper, seeded, thinly sliced
8-ounce package mushrooms, halved
1/2 cup chopped celery
10-ounce package frozen sweet peas
2 tablespoons butter
2 tablespoons flour
1/2 teaspoon seasoned salt
1/4 teaspoon dried sweet basil
1/4 teaspoon white pepper
3/4 cup half-and-half
1 tablespoon capers, drained

● Cook linguine according to directions on package; drain. Butter a 9 x 13-inch baking dish and evenly spread linguine over the bottom of the dish.

● Place veal strips over the linguine, overlapping if necessary. In a medium bowl, combine bell pepper, mushrooms, celery, and peas. Spoon over veal.

● In a small saucepan, over medium heat, melt butter; mix in flour and seasonings. Gradually stir in half-and-half.

● Cook, stirring constantly until mixture has thickened. Pour sauce over veal and vegetables. Top with capers. Bake covered at 350° for 40 minutes.

One-Dish Fish

Seafood Royale •

Crab Casserole •

Crabmeat Quiche •

Swiss Crab Casserole •

Crawfish Fettuccine •

Shrimp and Wild Rice en Cocotte •

Snow Pea Shrimp •

Shrimp Tetrazzini •

Sun-Dried Tomatoes and Shrimp •

Creole Chicken and Shrimp •

Shrimp Strata •

Cheesy Shrimp Casserole •

Shrimp and Artichokes •

Fresh Shrimp Pasta Bake •

• Shrimp Feta Flambé

• Baked Shrimp Gratinée

• Crackered Oysters

• Corn-Oyster Casserole

• Baked Oyster Casserole

• Seafood Baked Tomatoes

• Georgia Oyster Creole

• Flounder and Spinach Bake

• Sole with Mornay Sauce

• Seafood Medley Casserole

• Mediterranean Slow-Roasted Tuna

• Garlicky Fish Stew

• Fish and Vegetable Stew

• Savory Fish & Fennel Casserole

Seafood Royale

MAKES 6 SERVINGS

A meal on the wharf! Just add hot buttered French bread and a green salad. (And maybe a bottle of white wine—no dessert needed!)

1 cup uncooked rice

2 10¹/2-ounce cans cream of shrimp soup

3/4 cup milk

2/3 cup mayonnaise

1/4 teaspoon white pepper

1/2 teaspoon seasoned salt

1/2 teaspoon cayenne pepper

3 pounds cooked, peeled shrimp

6-ounce can crabmeat, drained

1 onion, chopped

2 cups chopped celery

4 tablespoons snipped parsley

5-ounce can sliced water chestnuts, drained

Slivered almonds

• Cook rice according to package directions until fluffy. Whisk together soup, milk, and mayonnaise until smooth and creamy.

• Add seasonings, shrimp, crabmeat, onion, celery, parsley, and water chestnuts. Stir in rice until well mixed. Add milk if dry.

• Pour into a lightly greased 9 x 13-inch baking dish and sprinkle almonds over top. Bake at 350° for 30 minutes or until heated thoroughly.

Crab Casserole

MAKES 4 SERVINGS

This crab casserole gives a luncheon a special touch when cooked in special pans known as ramekins. Ramekins are sometimes made of porcelain or earthenware—they really dress up your salad plate.

1/2 cup minced onion

1/4 cup minced celery

1/4 cup minced green bell pepper

1 clove garlic, minced

1 tablespoon chopped parsley

3/4 cup butter

2 cups soft bread crumbs

1/2 cup cream

1 hard-boiled egg, chopped

1 tablespoon white wine vinegar

1 teaspoon Worcestershire sauce

1/4 teaspoon thyme

1 teaspoon salt

Tabasco to taste

2 eggs, beaten

1 pound crabmeat, washed, picked over

Lemon

- In a skillet, sauté vegetables and parsley in 1/4 cup butter for 10 minutes or until tender. Add half the bread crumbs, cream, hard-boiled egg, vinegar, Worcestershire sauce, seasonings and Tabasco, mixing well. Add beaten eggs and crabmeat.

- Melt remaining butter and mix with remaining bread crumbs in separate bowl. Toss and reserve for topping. Pour crab mixture into individual lightly greased ramekins. Top with buttered crumbs.

- Bake in 1/4-inch deep hot water bath for 10 minutes or until crumbs are golden. Serve with lemon.

PREP TIME: 25 MINUTES   COOKING TIME: 40 MINUTES

Crabmeat Quiche

MAKES 6 SERVINGS

Lunch or brunch, Crabmeat Quiche is a winner!

6-ounce can crabmeat, drained

6 to 8 fresh mushrooms, sliced

2/3 cup chopped green onion

1/2 cup grated Swiss cheese

9-inch unbaked pie shell

2 eggs, beaten

1/2 cup milk

1/2 cup mayonnaise

2 tablespoons flour

1/2 teaspoon salt

1/2 stick butter, melted

● Flake crabmeat and remove shells. Combine crabmeat, mushrooms, green onion, and cheese, and place in pie shell.

● Combine eggs, milk, mayonnaise, flour, and salt, and beat well. Pour slowly over crabmeat. Add melted butter and bake at 350° for 40 minutes. Quiche is done when a knife inserted in the center comes out clean.

Swiss Crab Casserole

MAKES 6 SERVINGS

This hot crab dish can be served at a luncheon or a brunch—and really sets off those taste buds.

1 cup butter, melted

3 cups milk

1/2 teaspoon white pepper

6 eggs

1 cup biscuit mix

2 cups grated Swiss cheese

2 cups crabmeat

1 cup mayonnaise

• Mix butter, milk, white pepper, eggs, and biscuit mix in blender until smooth. Pour into a lightly greased 9 x 13-inch baking dish. Sprinkle with Swiss cheese.

• In a bowl, mix crabmeat with mayonnaise and spread on top of cheese, gently pressing down into liquid. Bake at 350° for 55 minutes. Remove from oven and let sit until firm.

Crawfish Fettuccine

MAKES 6 SERVINGS

This Crawfish Fettuccine will make you think you just flew into New Orleans.

12-ounce package fettuccine

3 bell peppers, chopped

3 onions, chopped

5 ribs celery, chopped

3 sticks butter

14-ounce package frozen crawfish tails

2 tablespoons snipped parsley

3 to 4 cloves garlic, minced

1 pint half-and-half

1/2 cup flour

1 pound jalapeño cheese, cubed

• Cook noodles according to directions. Drain and set aside. Sauté bell peppers, onions, and celery in butter.

• Add crawfish tails and simmer for 8 to 10 minutes, stirring occasionally. Add parsley, garlic, and half-and-half and mix well. Gradually stir in flour, mixing well.

• Simmer for 30 minutes, stirring occasionally. Add cheese and continue to stir until melted and blended. Mix fettuccine with sauce.

• Pour into a greased 6-quart baking dish. Bake at 300° for 15 to 20 minutes or until heated throughout.

PREP TIME: 25 MINUTES   COOKING TIME: 1 HOUR 35 MINUTES

Shrimp and Wild Rice en Cocotte

MAKES 6 SERVINGS

1 cup wild rice

5 1/4 cups chicken stock

1 onion, chopped

1 pound mushrooms, sliced

1 clove garlic, minced

1/4 cup butter

2 tablespoons flour

1/2 cup dry white wine

1/4 teaspoon salt

1/4 teaspoon pepper

1 teaspoon tarragon, crushed

1 1/2 pounds cooked shrimp, shelled, deveined

• Place rice and 4 cups stock in saucepan. Bring to boil. Simmer, covered, 45 to 50 minutes. Uncover. Fluff with fork. Simmer 5 minutes. Pour off any excess stock.

• Sauté onion, mushrooms, and garlic in butter, for 5 minutes. Add flour. Stir over medium heat 3 minutes. Add remaining stock and wine. Stir until slightly thickened. Add salt, pepper, and tarragon.

• Combine the rice-mushroom mixture and shrimp. Pour into a lightly greased 2-quart casserole. Bake covered at 350° for 30 minutes.

Snow Pea Shrimp

MAKES 6 SERVINGS

With pasta, shrimp, snow peas, and cheese, you can't go wrong.

3 cups penne pasta

1/2 cup butter

3 cloves garlic, minced

2 green onions, minced

2 cups sliced fresh mushrooms

1/2 cup flour

1/2 teaspoon salt

1/2 teaspoon pepper

15-ounce can chicken broth

2 cups milk

3 tablespoons dry white wine

3/4 cup grated Swiss cheese

2 1/4 cups frozen snow peas, thawed and drained

1 pound fresh shrimp, cleaned, cooked, peeled

1/2 cup grated Parmesan cheese

1/4 to 1/2 cup sliced almonds

● Cook and drain pasta according to package directions. In a large, deep skillet, melt butter and sauté garlic, onions, and mushrooms over low heat. Continue cooking until mushrooms are tender; stir occasionally.

● Add flour, salt, and pepper, stirring constantly over medium heat. Stir until all lumps are disolved and sauce is smooth and bubbly. Gradually stir in broth, milk, and wine and stir continuously until smooth.

● Turn heat to high, bring sauce to a boil, and stir in Swiss cheese. Stir until cheese is melted and remove from heat. Add snow peas, shrimp, and pasta to mushroom mixture and stir to mix well.

● Pour into a lightly greased 9 x 13-inch baking dish. Sprinkle Parmesan and almonds over top. Bake at 350° for 20 to 25 minutes or until golden brown.

PREP TIME: 30 MINUTES   COOKING TIME: 40 MINUTES

Shrimp Tetrazzini

MAKES 4 SERVINGS

This is not your ordinary Tetrazzini—shrimp makes it top-notch company fare.

1 stick butter
4 green onions with tops, chopped
1 cup water
5 tablespoons flour
2 1/2 cups chicken broth
1/2 cup clam juice
1/2 cup white wine
1/2 cup cooking sherry
1/2 cup cream
1/2 teaspoon oregano
1 cup grated Parmesan cheese, plus extra for topping
2 tablespoons oil
1 pound mushrooms, sliced
1/2 teaspoon garlic salt
8 ounces spaghetti
2 pounds shrimp, cooked, shelled, deveined
1/2 teaspoon salt
1/4 teaspoon pepper

• In a skillet, melt half the butter. Add green onions and water and bring to a boil. Reduce heat and simmer until water has boiled away and only the butter remains and onions are soft.

• Stir in flour until smooth and cook for about 3 minutes. Do not brown. Add broth, clam juice, wine, sherry, cream, and oregano. Cook, stirring constantly with a whisk, until sauce begins to boil. Stir in 1 cup grated cheese and set aside.

• Melt remaining butter with oil over high heat. Sauté mushrooms and garlic salt until brown, about 4 minutes.

• Cook spaghetti according to package directions; drain.

• Mix sauce, mushooms, and spaghetti with shrimp and season with salt and pepper. Pour into a lightly greased 3-quart baking dish and top with Parmesan cheese. Bake uncovered at 375° for 15 to 20 minutes or until sauce bubbles and is brown.

Sun-Dried Tomatoes and Shrimp

MAKES 6 SERVINGS

This casserole features superb flavor and shrimp at its finest.

1 pound shrimp, cleaned

1 tablespoon pickling spice

1 teaspoon salt, divided

1 pound spaghetti

1 1/2 cups small-curd cottage cheese, drained

12-ounce can evaporated milk

2 cloves garlic, minced

1/2 teaspoon white pepper

1/4 teaspoon red pepper flakes

2 tablespoons extra-virgin olive oil

1 cup sun-dried tomatoes, chopped

4 ounces feta cheese

1 cup chopped fresh basil leaves

1/4 cup chopped fresh parsley

● In a large pot, cover shrimp with water, season with pickling spice, and bring to a boil. Cook just until shrimp are pink.

● Remove shrimp from water and drain. Set aside. Rinse pot and fill with water. Bring to a boil; add 1/2 teaspoon salt and spaghetti. Cook spaghetti until al dente, drain, and set aside.

● In a blender, combine cottage cheese, evaporated milk, garlic, 1/2 teaspoon salt, pepper, and red pepper flakes, and process on high until well blended. Continue processing on high and slowly pour oil in blender until well blended.

● Pour mixture into large saucepan and cook on low heat, stirring constantly. Do not boil. Slowly add shrimp, continue stirring until slightly thickened. Remove from heat.

● Put spaghetti in serving bowl and pour sauce-shrimp mixture over spaghetti. Toss to mix. Add sun-dried tomatoes, feta cheese, and basil and toss again. Garnish with fresh parsley.

Creole Chicken and Shrimp

MAKES 6 SERVINGS

The best of the culinary world!

1 tablespoon pickling spice

1 1/2 pounds shrimp, peeled and deveined

4 tablespoons olive oil

4 boneless, skinless chicken breast halves

1 bunch green onions and tops, chopped

1/2 cup chopped celery

1/3 cup chopped red bell pepper

1/3 cup chopped green bell pepper

8-ounce can tomato sauce

1/2 cup white wine

1/4 teaspoon Tabasco sauce

1 tablespoon Worcestershire sauce

2 to 3 tablespoons snipped parsley

1/4 teaspoon thyme

1 1/2 teaspoons salt

1/2 teaspoon pepper

1 cup half-and-half

rice

● Fill large pot three-quaters full with water and bring to a boil. Add pickling spice and shrimp and cook just until shrimp turn pink. Remove shrimp, drain, and chill.

● In a large skillet, heat oil and brown chicken on both sides, and sauté until centers are no longer pink. Remove from skillet and drain on paper towel. Cool and cut into bite-size pieces.

● Put onions, celery, and bell peppers in the skillet and sauté until onion is translucent. Add chicken to skillet and stir in tomato sauce, white wine, Tabasco, Worcestershire sauce, parsley, thyme, salt, and pepper, and mix well.

● Pour into a lightly greased 4-quart baking dish and bake at 350° for 40 to 45 minutes. Remove chicken dish and stir in shrimp and half-and-half. Bake until heated throughout. Serve over rice.

PREP TIME: 20 MINUTES (REFRIGERATE OVERNIGHT)   COOKING TIME: 45 MINUTES

Shrimp Strata

MAKES 6 SERVINGS

Leftover ham can be substituted for the shrimp.

Butter, softened
5 slices white bread
10 to 12 ounces fresh shrimp, cooked, cut in
*   bite-size pieces*
8-ounce package shredded Cheddar cheese
2 tablespoons dried flaked onions
3 eggs, beaten
1 1/2 cups half-and-half
1/2 teaspoon seasoned salt
1/4 teaspoon white pepper
1 teaspoon dry mustard
Paprika

● Spread the softened butter over the 5 slices of white bread. Cut into 1-inch cubes.

● Butter a 9 x 13-inch baking dish and place half the bread cubes over bottom of dish. Layer half the shrimp and cheese. Make one more layer of the bread cubes, shrimp, and cheese, then sprinkle flaked onions over top.

● In a bowl, combine the eggs, half-and-half, salt, pepper, and mustard; mix well. Pour over layered mixture.

● Cover and let set in the refrigerator overnight or at least for 4 to 5 hours. Bake uncovered at 325° for 45 minutes. Cool for 5 to 10 minutes before serving. Garnish with paprika.

PREP TIME: 15 MINUTES   COOKING TIME: 40 MINUTES

Cheesy Shrimp Casserole

MAKES 6 SERVINGS

Wow—these three cheeses and the salsa make this shrimp dish a 10!

8-ounce package angel hair pasta

8-ounce package shredded Swiss cheese

8-ounce package feta cheese, crumbled

8-ounce carton plain yogurt

1 cup evaporated milk

4 eggs

1/2 cup fresh parsley, snipped

1 teaspoon basil

1 teaspoon oregano

3 cloves garlic, minced

16-ounce jar chunky salsa

1 pound uncooked shrimp, peeled and deveined

16-ounce package grated mozzarella cheese

● Cook pasta according to directions on package, drain, and set aside. Preheat oven to 350°.

● In large mixing bowl, combine the Swiss and feta cheeses, yogurt, milk, eggs, parsley, basil, oregano, and garlic.

● In a lightly greased 9 x 13-inch baking dish, spread half the pasta, half the cheese mixture, half the salsa and half the shrimp in layers. Repeat layers using all remaining pasta, cheese mixture, salsa, and shrimp.

● Sprinkle top with mozzarella and bake 350° for 30 to 40 minutes or until heated throughout. Cool slightly before serving.

PREP TIME: 10 MINUTES COOKING TIME: 40 MINUTES

Shrimp and Artichokes

MAKES 6 SERVINGS

To make this casserole ahead of time, cover before you sprinkle with cheese, and refrigerate until ready to bake. Sprinkle with cheese just before baking.

1 onion, chopped

3 ribs of celery, chopped

2 cloves garlic, finely minced

2 red bell peppers, chopped

1 green bell pepper, chopped

2/3 stick butter

3 pounds shrimp, boiled, peeled and deveined

3 1/2 cups cooked white rice

1/2 cup tomato sauce

8-ounce carton heavy cream

1/2 to 3/4 teaspoon red pepper

1/2 teaspoon seasoned salt

2 14-ounce cans artichoke hearts, drained and halved

2 cups shredded Cheddar cheese

● In a large skillet, sauté onion, celery, garlic, and bell peppers in the butter. Add cooked shrimp and rice, mixing well. Add tomato sauce, cream, red pepper, salt, and artichoke hearts; mix well.

● Pour into a buttered 9 x 13-inch baking dish. Sprinkle with cheese and bake at 350° for 30 minutes, or until ingredients are thoroughly heated.

PREP TIME: 20 MINUTES   COOKING TIME: 45 MINUTES

Fresh Shrimp Pasta Bake

MAKES 6 SERVINGS

The richness of this pasta dish gives a creamy, delightful taste that blends well with shrimp.

2 pounds shrimp, shelled and deveined

1/2 cup butter

8-ounce package spinach linguine

1 cup sour cream

1 cup mayonnaise

10 1/2-ounce cream of mushroom soup

1 teaspoon Dijon mustard

1/4 cup dry sherry

1 tablespoon minced fresh chives

3/4 cup shredded sharp Cheddar cheese

- In large skillet, sauté shrimp in butter for 3 to 5 minutes, stirring often. Remove from heat and set aside.

- Cook pasta until al dente. Drain and place evenly in a lightly greased 9 x 13-inch baking dish. Pour shrimp over pasta and spread out in a second layer.

- In a separate bowl, combine sour cream, mayonnaise, mushroom soup, mustard, sherry, and chives. Mix thoroughly and pour over shrimp and pasta.

- Spread cheese on top of mixture and bake at 350° for 30 minutes.

PREP TIME: 20 MINUTES   COOKING TIME: 1 HOUR

Shrimp Feta Flambé

MAKES 6 SERVINGS

This dramatic presentation will impress the most sophisticated of guests, even if the flame is a small one. The higher the alcohol content of the liquor added, the higher the flame.

1 white onion, chopped

2 ribs celery, sliced

1/2 cup olive oil

15-ounce can diced tomatoes

4-ounce can chopped green chilies

2 tablespoons chopped, fresh cilantro

1/2 teaspoon seasoned salt

1/2 teaspoon cayenne pepper

2 cloves garlic, minced

21/2 pounds shrimp, lightly cooked, peeled and
    deveined

1/2 pound feta cheese

1/4 cup vodka

Hot cooked white rice

● In a large saucepan, sauté onion and celery in oil until transparent. Add tomatoes, green chilies, cilantro, salt, cayenne pepper, and garlic. Cover and simmer for 45 minutes.

● Add shrimp to sauce and spoon into a buttered 3-quart baking dish. Crumble cheese over shrimp.

● Bake uncovered at 350° for 10 to 15 minutes. Remove from oven. When ready to serve, pour heated vodka over shrimp and flame. Serve over hot white rice.

PREP TIME: 5 MINUTES   COOKING TIME: 30 MINUTES

Baked Shrimp Gratinée

MAKES 4 SERVINGS

Gratinée refers to dishes topped with cheese, bread-crumbs, and butter slices and heated.

1/2 cup butter, softened

3 teaspoons garlic salt, divided

2 1/2 to 3 pounds cooked shrimp, shelled and deveined

1 cup grated Parmesan cheese, divided

1 quart small-curd cottage cheese, undrained

1 cup cracker crumbs

1/4 cup butter, sliced

1 1/2 cups slivered almonds, toasted

● Spread butter mixed with 1 teaspoon garlic salt over sides and bottom of 3-quart baking dish. Spread layer of shrimp on bottom and sprinkle with 1 teaspoon garlic salt and 1/2 cup Parmesan cheese.

● Make a second layer of cottage cheese on top of shrimp, and again sprinkle with 1 teaspoon garlic salt and remaining Parmesan cheese.

● Top with cracker crumbs, then butter slices and finally almonds. Bake at 350° for 25 to 30 minutes.

Crackered Oysters

MAKES 6 SERVINGS

Oyster lovers, come and get it!

2 pints fresh oysters
2 tablespoons fresh lemon juice
1/2 cup melted butter
2 cups crumbled Saltine crackers, divided
Cracked black pepper
1/2 pint half-and-half
1/2 teaspoon Worcestershire sauce
1/2 teaspoon salt
2 teaspoons dry white wine

• Drain oysters and reserve liquid. Combine lemon juice and melted butter and stir to mix. Pour over cracker crumbs, stir, and toss to mix.

• In a lightly greased 9 x 13-inch baking dish, spread one third of the cracker crumbs over bottom of dish. Layer half the oysters and repeat with another third of the cracker crumbs and remaining oysters.

• Lightly grind cracked black pepper over oysters. Mix together reserved oyster liquid and enough half-and-half to equal one cup.

• Stir in Worcestershire sauce, salt, and wine. Pour over oysters and sprinkle remaining cracker crumbs over top.

• Bake at 350° for 30 minutes or until well heated.

Corn-Oyster Casserole

MAKES 4 SERVINGS

Invite the neighbors for a Saturday night supper. This casserole is easy to make and will be a surprising new dish!

1 quart oysters, drained, quartered
2 15-ounce cans cream-style corn
1/2 cup evaporated milk
1 teaspoon salt
1/2 teaspoon pepper
1/8 teaspoon Tabasco sauce
3 cups crumbled Saltine crackers
1 cup butter, melted

• In a bowl, mix oysters with corn, milk, salt, pepper, and Tabasco. Add crackers to melted butter and spread in a lightly greased baking dish. Top with oyster mixture.

• Bake at 350° for 40 minutes.

Baked Oyster Creole

MAKES 6 SERVINGS

Celery, bell pepper, green onions, and garlic are staples in Louisiana dishes and this recipe is no exception. Similar to a stuffing, this oyster dish can be served as a casserole side dish at any meal.

1 cup butter

1 1/4 cups minced celery

1 green or red bell pepper, diced

1 bunch fresh green onions with tops, diced

3 cloves garlic, minced

1 cup heavy cream

2 pints oysters in liquid

1 tablespoon hot sauce

2 tablespoons Worcestershire sauce

1 teaspoon salt

3 eggs, hard-boiled, chopped

3 cups seasoned dry bread crumbs

- In a heavy saucepan, melt butter over moderate heat and sauté celery, bell pepper, onions, and garlic several minutes until all appear translucent and tender.

- Slowly pour in heavy cream, stirring constantly. Bring to almost boiling, and reduce heat. Continue stirring and add oysters with their liquid and cook until oysters have curled.

- Remove from heat and add hot sauce, Worcestershire sauce, salt, and eggs. Pour in 1 cup bread crumbs and stir. Continue adding bread crumbs and stir until consistency is moist, but firm enough to hold its shape.

- Spoon into a lightly greased 9 x 13-inch baking dish and bake at 350° for 50 to 60 minutes.

PREP TIME: 20 MINUTES   COOKING TIME: 45 MINUTES

Seafood Baked Tomatoes

MAKES 6 SERVINGS

Here's a quick casserole that looks stunning. Feel free to use canned crabmeat or shrimp if you don't have fresh on hand.

6 large, firm tomatoes

Salt

2 tablespoons butter

4 tablespoons minced green onions and tops

4 tablespoons minced celery

4 tablespoons minced green or red bell pepper

1 1/2 tablespoons flour

1 1/2 cups milk

1 1/2 cups crabmeat, chopped lobster, or shrimp

2 teaspoons Worcestershire sauce

1/2 teaspoon cayenne pepper

1/2 teaspoon salt

1 cup grated Cheddar cheese

Lettuce

Green onions with tops

Radishes

Celery with leaves

Parsley

● Preheat oven to 350°. Hollow out tomatoes from stem end, leaving enough meat to hold shape of tomato. Hollow out enough area to fill with seafood mixture for one serving. Lightly salt inside of tomatoes and invert on rack to drain for about 15 minutes.

● In a skillet, melt butter and sauté onions, celery, and green pepper until tender and translucent. Stir in flour and whisk until smooth and all lumps are dissolved. Slowly stir in milk, stirring constantly.

● Continue cooking and stirring until sauce has thickened to gravy consistency. Add seafood of choice and continue to stir. Add Worcestershire sauce, cayenne, salt, and cheese and stir until cheese has melted. Remove from heat.

● Put tomato shells in a lightly greased baking dish, closed side down, and spoon in filling. If tomatoes are ripe and shells don't hold their shape very well, put tomato shells in well-buttered muffin tins. Put baking dish in a roasting pan containing several inches of water and place in oven. Bake at 350° for 20 minutes. Serve on a bed of lettuce and garnish with green onions, radishes, celery, and parsley.

Georgia Oyster Creole

MAKES 6 SERVINGS

Maybe you'll find a pearl!

2 quarts oysters
1 stick butter, divided
4 whole scallions, chopped
1 cup chopped green or red bell pepper
1 1/2 cups sliced mushrooms
1/4 cup flour
1 cup heavy cream
1/3 cup grated parmesan cheese
Freshly grated nutmeg
1/2 teaspoon paprika
Salt to taste
Freshly ground black pepper
3/4 cup bread crumbs

• Drain the oysters and set aside. In a large skillet, melt 2 tablespoons butter. Add scallions and bell pepper and sauté until the vegetables are tender. Add mushrooms and oysters and sauté for 5 minutes.

• In a separate pan, melt 2 tablespoons of the remaining butter over medium low heat. Add flour, stirring constantly until smooth. Add the cream and stir constantly until bubbling and thick.

• Mix in cheese, then pour cheese sauce into the oyster mixture and season with nutmeg, paprika, salt, and pepper. Let simmer 3 to 5 minutes.

• Pour the mixture into a sprayed 9 x 13-inch baking dish, top with bread crumbs, and dot with the remaining butter. Place under the broiler until browned and bubbling, about 10 minutes.

Flounder and Spinach Bake

MAKES 6 TO 8 SERVINGS

The fresh taste of flounder is enhanced by spinach and mushrooms.

2 10-ounce packages frozen chopped spinach

8-ounce carton sour cream

1/2 onion, finely chopped

1/2 red bell pepper, chopped

2 tablespoons flour

2 tablespoons lemon juice

1 tablespoon heavy cream

1/4 teaspoon pepper

1/4 teaspoon seasoned salt

6 to 8 flounder fillets

2/3 cup fresh sliced mushrooms

Paprika

● Cook spinach according to package directions. Drain very well. In a bowl, combine sour cream, onion, bell pepper, flour, lemon juice, cream, pepper, and seasoned salt, mixing well.

● Add half of the mixture to the spinach, mixing well. Place spinach mixture in a 9 x 13-inch buttered baking dish. Arrange flounder on top of spinach. Place mushrooms around flounder.

● Top with remaining sour cream mixture and sprinkle with paprika. Bake at 375° for 15 to 20 minutes or until fish flakes easily.

PREP TIME: 10 MINUTES   COOKING TIME: 30 MINUTES

Sole with Mornay Sauce

MAKES 6 TO 8 SERVINGS

This is an exceptional dish for any full-flavored fish. With all its rich and creamy texture, select a fish that can stand up to this special sauce.

6 to 8 filets of sole
Salt
Pepper
White wine
1/2 stick butter
1/4 cup flour
2 cups half-and-half
1 cup grated Swiss cheese
Grated Parmesan cheese

● Place sole in a large skillet. Sprinkle with salt and pepper; pour in enough white wine to just barely cover fish. Cook until fish flakes easily when tested with fork.

● Carefully remove fish to a shallow, lightly greased baking dish and keep warm. In a saucepan, melt butter and add flour, stirring well. Add half-and-half to the butter and flour mixture, stirring well.

● Cook (do not boil), stirring vigorously, until sauce is smooth and creamy. Remove sauce from heat and let cool several minutes. Stir in the Swiss cheese.

● Pour sauce over fish and sprinkle with Parmesan cheese. Place in a very hot oven (about 425°) and bake about 10 minutes or until cheese begins to glaze.

PREP TIME: 10 MINUTES   COOKING TIME: 35 MINUTES

Seafood Medley Casserole

MAKES 6 SERVINGS

Fresh crabmeat, scallops, and shrimp are good anytime, but when served over your favorite ribbon pastas, they become a special treat for special occasions.

1 pound crabmeat

1 pound scallops, thoroughly cleaned

1 pound shrimp, shelled and deveined

6 eggs, hard-boiled, chopped

2 cups heavy cream

3/4 cup shredded Swiss cheese

2 tablespoons flour

1 teaspoon dry mustard

1 teaspoon salt

1 teaspoon white pepper

1/3 to 1/2 cup milk (optional)

2 1-pound packages fettuccine, linguine, or pappardelle pasta

- In a buttered 9 x 13-inch baking dish, place uncooked crabmeat, scallops, and shrimp. Sprinkle chopped egg on top of seafood and set aside.

- In a heavy saucepan over moderate heat, heat cream almost to boiling. Remove from heat and stir in Swiss cheese. Continue to stir until cheese melts.

- In a separate dish, mix together flour, mustard, salt, and pepper and pour into cream and cheese mixture. As sauce is stirred it will thicken slightly. If sauce thickens beyond thin, add up to 1/2 cup milk to thin.

- Pour sauce over seafood and bake at 350° for 30 to 35 minutes. Serve over pasta cooked until al dente.

PREP TIME: 20 MINUTES   COOKING TIME: 40 MINUTES

Mediterranean Slow-Roasted Tuna

MAKES 6 SERVINGS

2¹/2-pound sashimi-grade tuna fillet

10 whole cloves

10 whole coriander seeds

3 large garlic cloves, very thinly sliced

Salt and freshly ground black pepper to taste

1/4 cup extra-virgin olive oil

1 large red onion, thinly sliced

1¹/2 pounds plum tomatoes, halved, seeded, and
   chopped

1 teaspoon dried oregano

1/3 cup white wine vinegar

• Preheat oven to 200°. Make 10 slits around the sides of the tuna filet. Place 1 clove, 1 coriander seed, and 1 slice of garlic in each of the slits. Season the tuna with salt and pepper.

• In an ovenproof pot, heat oil over medium heat. Sauté onion 8 minutes and then push to one side of the pot. Add tuna and sear until brown on all sides, about 10 to 12 minutes. Mix tuna and onions. Add tomatoes, oregano, and remaining garlic slices, sprinkling around the tuna. Season with salt and pepper to taste and drizzle vinegar over the fish.

• Bake uncovered until tuna is medium-rare, about 20 minutes. Transfer the tuna to a serving platter and slice thin. Spoon the tomato sauce over the tuna and serve.

PREP TIME: 10 MINUTES   COOKING TIME: 10 MINUTES

Savory Fish & Fennel Casserole

MAKES 6 SERVINGS

2 *pounds monkfish or mullet fillets, approximately*
   1/2-inch thick

1 *medium fennel bulb trimmed, quartered and*
   thinly sliced

2 *tablespoons orange juice*

2 *tablespoons soy sauce*

1 *tablespoon onion, finely chopped*

2 *teaspoons ground oregano*

1 *teaspoon freshly ground black pepper*

3-*ounce can tomato paste*

- Set oven to broil.

- Place fillets in a lightly greased glass casserole dish. Sprinkle fennel slices around the fish. Combine orange juice, soy sauce, onion, oregano, and pepper and pour over fillets. Broil for 5 minutes, until fillets and fennel start to turn golden brown; remove from oven. Drain and reserve liquid. Combine reserved liquid, tomato paste, and 1/2 cup water. Pour over fillets and fennel.

- Return casserole to oven and bake at 350° for 5 minutes or until mixture is bubbling.

- Remove from oven and let rest for 10 minutes.

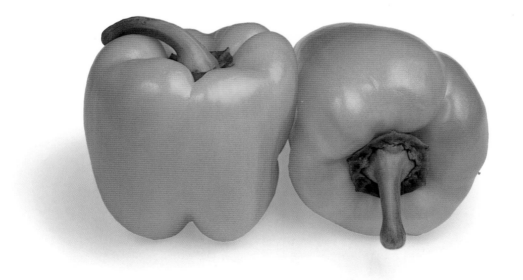

Index